MY BLUEPRINT

Mirror My Healing Steps and Thrive

BY

Jocelyne Chidiac

DEDICATION

To my children, Gaelle and Shawn, who inspired me to write this book a few years ago. I offer it to you both with all my heart. Thank you for choosing me as your mom, friend, and therapist. You are both my therapists, and I am honored and proud to be your mom.

To my siblings, Elie, Micha, and Tony, who always stood by me and supported me, especially during the toughest times of my life.

To my parents, who showed us strength, courage, resilience, and hope through their actions. While they were sometimes too conservative and had many rules, these experiences shaped my personality and character as an adult.

To everyone who touched my life positively – my teachers, bosses, healers, mentors, colleagues, countless friends (you are too many to name), and my ever-growing list of clients who helped me heal even more by allowing me to help you heal and change your lives.

And to those who triggered me, pushed my buttons, and affected me negatively – the pain you caused me led to my own healing.

Some of you have left this world, and others are still here. To all of you, I am grateful for the experiences. I forgive you and myself for allowing you to hurt me at some point. You are the reason I sought healing and, eventually, healed.

TABLE OF CONTENTS

INTRODUCTION

This book will reveal the transformative power of healing, forgiveness, love, resilience, compassion, gratitude and much more.

Through carefully curated exercises and stories drawn from my real-life experiences and historical periods, you will understand how these qualities significantly shape and influence our lives.

Each story and lesson is intended to show you not just the challenges but also the strength you draw from overcoming them and the lessons you learn by facing them.

The exercises in this book blend my personal practices and the wisdom I have gathered from my healing journey.

After reading hundreds of books and receiving invaluable advice from mentors and teachers, I have compiled what I believe to be the most effective tools for personal growth and healing. These exercises are designed to guide you inward, to help you connect with yourself, and to unlock the amazing natural ability of healing we all have.

CHAPTER 1
Dubai – 2024

Life in the big city runs rampant, roaring through the streets as time boasts of its endless march. The ordeal is hectic and chaotic, but as I sit in my serene and peaceful garden, the droning sound of Dubai's morning hustle fades to the point where it is no longer a background sound in my story.

In these moments of tranquillity and quietness, my mind wanders the street of time, and I recall the journey of life that has brought me to 2024.

The garden around me is teeming with life and the energy of vibrant colors. The textures of plants and their flowers signal a hundred new possibilities and probabilities today.

Even though calm, a lot is happening in these moments of tranquility. The fragrance of flowers and plants and the earthy smell of soil triggers a primordial feeling. This feeling hints at the interconnectedness of all life on the planet and the divinity of being one with beautiful nature.

The air is rejuvenating and refreshing, but I know the desert sun will soon bring warmth, a herald of new starts, infinite energy and unlimited potential.

Outside, towering glass skyscrapers of Dubai are reaching the sky, reflecting the morning sun and creating a breathtaking display of light and shadow.

Inside, my garden walls overflow with Bougainvillea flowers in stunning hues of pink and orange.

I have intentionally nurtured a sense of inner peace here. Time seems to stand still in my garden, offering a reflective escape from the fast-paced urban life, and this is where I find the connection to my inner being.

This connection reminds me of the motivation that brought me to where I am now. It reminds me of the balance I have achieved between external chaos and internal serenity.

Being in touch with my inner being gives me direction and the strength to overcome challenges the day brings.

As the city slowly comes to life, I am reminded of the significance of nurturing inner peace amid external stresses.

Maintaining and nurturing this quiet space amidst the world's chaos has become my regular practice.

I always wanted a frangipani tree in my garden. I used to visit my ex-husband's office, which had two big frangipani trees at the entrance, and I always said I would love to have them in my garden someday.

Fast forward to 2024; I now have two frangipani trees—one huge in front of my house and the other inside the courtyard, blooming most of the year with beautiful white flowers that drive me to always dream of better days to come.

Sitting here looking at these flowers, I can't help but smile, thinking about how this simple wish from years ago came true.

I fulfilled this and many more desires, proving that the universe and the Creator make our wishes come true. All we have to do is ask the universe passionately and then let go.

You'll be surprised to witness these wishes come true when you least anticipate them.

And so many of my wishes came true, but that does not mean I did not go through my fair share of hurdles and difficulties.

Numerous difficulties accompanied me for most of my adult years spent in Dubai. You need to know that I got here at the ripe age of 22. Currently, I am 58 years old.

In the past, I often wondered if I would ever catch a break from all the suffering or if my troubles were destined to follow me until the end of my days.

Deep down inside, I knew that I was the only person to be blamed for my unhappiness, and I was the creator of these troubles myself, but I always overlooked this fact.

I didn't realize this fully until the day when I finally took the time to dig deep into my soul. I then understood that life can be happy if I see it that way. I also realized that in our twenties and thirties, we feel like we have plenty of time to accomplish our dreams, travel to foreign and new countries, achieve goals, and reach all our aspirations, but when we reach our fifties, we quickly realize how brief life is and suddenly our priorities and perspective shifts.

Living in Dubai provided a one-of-a-kind setting for my path of self-exploration. I had a demanding job and a business that was difficult to run. I split with my ex-husband when my daughter was eight and a half years old and my son was two and a half years old. I brought them up all by myself, and my heart swells with pride at seeing that they have graduated from their universities and are successful in their professions.

I did not have family in the UAE except for a few friends who became my family and some people I met who became great friends. Fortunate circumstances made these amazing people a part of my journey. These people contributed significantly to my achievements, healing, and renewed faith in myself and LIFE.

While it's true that Dubai took numerous things from me - my marriage, my youth, my time, my money- it is also a fact that it gave me so much more.

It provided me protection for my kids, a sense of self, and all the encounters that shaped me into the healed individual I am now. It truly is a fact that fills me with pride and joy.

Dubai provided me with dreams that I turned into reality. It provided me with opportunities, some of which I seized and profited from while others I overlooked. Most of all, Dubai gave my children and me a 'Home.'

I found a spot in this city and decided to renovate and develop it into my own sanctuary. My personal garden is my source of stability, always reminding me of the experiences that have shaped me and my future.

How did I achieve what I desired?

What did I do to make it happen?

How did I move from struggling to thriving?

For these answers, you will need to stick around and keep reading.

So, after all the experiences, failures, successes, heartbreaks, and moments of joy, I can look at myself in the mirror and proudly say that I am self-sufficient.

I stand as a woman who has experienced and harnessed the power of meditation, journaling, discipline, setting goals, and Jin Shin Jyutsu!

My healing and progress is not limited to myself. I help others, too. I assist thousands of individuals from various backgrounds and all walks of life, including men, women, teenagers, little ones, and whole families, in healing, enhancing and transforming their lives for the better.

Under my supervision and guidance, people transition from severe depression to embracing a transformed life filled with goals, optimism, and inner peace. They heal from whatever trauma ailed them and value themselves, attracting financial freedom and admiration.

Children have a hard time expressing and finding out what troubles them. I assist shy children with learning difficulties and low self-esteem in getting their confidence and spark back. A kid's childhood shapes them into the adult they become, and no child should suffer the way many do due to the lack of proper care and attention.

My profession is defined by everything I have learned and utilized for my healing, with a special emphasis on Jin Shin Jyutsu.

This opening chapter is not just a recount of my present-day life but an image of the path of healing and evolution that led me here to you.

Before moving forward, let's rewind my childhood years to understand how it all began. Looking back at our childhood, we can begin to understand where our beliefs, fears, and habits come from, and with that understanding comes the power to change them. This journey toward 'unprogramming' ourselves is one of the most important steps we can take for a better, more fulfilling tomorrow.

EXERCISE

Acceptance is the key.

First and foremost, acknowledge that you need help and healing. This way, you are not only making way for solutions to come your way but also communicating with the universe.

Once you have acknowledged this fact, look for the right healers and modality of healing for you and then dedicate all your time, energy, and finances to it.

You deserve this, and things will only get better when you do!

If you don't take action for yourself, no one else will do it for you. Your life belongs to you, and you have the sole authority to make any changes you desire.

Next, get yourself a nice notebook, diary or journal and jot down your emotions and feelings. Note down the date and location you are currently at, then allow your hand to express your thoughts on paper freely.

If you feel stuck at any moment, write the sentence, "What would it take for me to express myself now? What would it take for me to clear my thoughts now?" and then take a deep breath and give it a go. You will start writing again smoothly.

We will be doing more exercises at the end of every chapter. Once you complete the book and the exercises in each chapter, you will be able to change your frequency, raise your vibrational energy, and improve various aspects of your life significantly.

TESTIMONIALS

"I came to Jocelyne during one of the lowest points in my life, struggling with both health issues and personal losses. Her compassionate approach and deep understanding of the healing arts were instrumental in my recovery. More than just healing my body, she helped me heal my spirit, for which I will be forever thankful."

LESSON 1

It all starts with acknowledging your experiences, including the relationships and people who have supported you. It is important to show appreciation to those who have supported you and provided you with care and peace.

Recognizing their constant support through life's difficulties highlights the power of human connection.

Negative experiences and people who have hurt you teach you as much as anyone else. It is just as important to forgive them, too.

Keeping repressed anger can weigh you down and eat you from the inside. Forgiveness is not about approving the harm caused. It is about letting go of the negative feelings associated with the past and welcoming the future with a clear head and conscience.

Every positive or negative event contributes to your personal development and recovery. Just as a phoenix rises from its ashes, you can become stronger and wiser with every obstacle you conquer.

The ability to heal lies in gaining wisdom from your past, applying it to the present and stepping into the future as a better and improved person.

Accepting and embracing challenges and situations as they are and showing gratitude and forgiveness can unearth a deeper sense of purpose and inner peace.

My life adventure highlights how people can grow and succeed, and this adventure can begin right now at your whim.

Explore your values and passions to understand what drives you. Practice self-love and set meaningful goals. Celebrate your achievements and use setbacks as learning opportunities. Practice activities such as mindfulness, exercise, artistic expression, and spending time in nature with family and friends to promote healing.

You will build resilience, enhance your quality of life, nurture significant connections, and achieve satisfaction.

This healing method will help boost your strength, enhance your relationships, strengthen your bond with the universe, and bring significance to your life. Have confidence in your intuition, and understand that peace and serenity are already present inside you, ready to be embraced.

CHAPTER 2

Childhood

The beginning of my story takes place in the peaceful outskirts of Beirut, Lebanon, during the 1960s. It was a location where tradition and modernity coexisted, creating a life that was rich in culture.

The essence of our community lay in the daily sounds of joy that filled the air. The happiness and contentment permeated from the delightful smell of fresh bread from the ovens and the earthy petrichor after each rain, signaling the beginning of a new day or season.

Our family residence was not just a building made of bricks and mortar but a sanctuary filled with unconditional love. The walls of this house were painted in friendly and welcoming ways, containing memories that would soon influence the person I would become.

At the heart of the house was the large kitchen where my mother ruled with her cooking skills. It was where basic ingredients from my maternal grandfather's garden were used to create meals that provided warmth to the soul and solace to the heart.

I remember the delicious smell of 'kibbeh' cooking in the oven, its fragrance bringing the family around the wooden table. This wooden table had seen numerous meals we enjoyed together, not only with the delicious food but also through sharing historical stories, light-hearted laughter, and the joy of companionship.

Every meal my mom made was like an homage to our culture, a festive mix of tastes that connected us to our forebears and the traditions they established long ago.

You see, I was born into a big family. The family was rich, with relatives on both my mother's and father's sides, and our homes settled close to each other, which meant that our doors were always open and the lines between these households were blurred thin.

While growing up, this closeness turned every occasion into a large family gathering and the simplest events into grand celebrations. I had become used to it. Because of this, I learned the value of community and the strength of family ties from a very young age. Our frequent interactions weren't just about fun; they were about giving priority to the family. Each holiday or weekend dinner was an opportunity for all of us to bond, share stories, and build memories.

In this loving and supportive environment filled with so many family members, I wasn't just growing up in terms of age but also in terms of wisdom. Opinions, culture and experiences from many generations were influencing me.

Whether it was something I overheard, something taught to us directly, or even lessons from school, these experiences, deeply rooted in my familial closeness, taught me that family always comes first and every challenge is faced collectively.

I recall our home being a mosaic of creative space, with each corner holding memories. My one-story house was located beside my dad's oldest brother's house. Both our families used the grand entrance of our two houses.

I always loved nature and trees, and when no one was looking, I enjoyed climbing the big rubber tree in front of our houses. We also grew various kinds of grapes - black, red, and white - in the rooftop vineyard and the back garden.

The family room in my childhood house, with its comfy sofas and the expansive rug, felt like a haven. It was where my mother would bring us together on stormy nights, the sound of rain hitting the windows as a background to the stories we listened to all night. She told tales of our ancestors and stories infused with the magic and wisdom of our culture, using a voice that could control the oceans and murmur to the stars. We would gather on the rug around her, eating popcorn or grilled chestnuts and listening to the stories that always end with, "And this is the story I told you, and in your chest, I hide it," as she used to say in Arabic.

Even though small, the garden was our domain, where my siblings and I reigned supreme, letting our creativity soar amidst the fig trees, mulberry trees, and jasmine bushes.

This humble garden saw our youthful games, our secret agreements, and the many hours we spent reclining on the grass, observing the clouds moving across the canopy of vines and leaves that obscure the sky but offer glimpses of the clouds elsewhere between the flora.

In this garden, I initially discovered the life cycles, the constant growth and change that affect all living beings. I learned valuable lessons from the elders through basic actions such as caring for plants and observing their blossoming.

You must know that in my youth, my family and I had to relocate multiple times, moving from one city to another. I had to adapt to numerous aspects of this lifestyle. Living a nomadic lifestyle like this resulted in me going to four different schools, with each relocation introducing me to unique cultures and new neighborhoods each time.

Naturally, these frequent alterations greatly impacted my growth, introducing me to varied social settings and instilling adaptability from a young age.

Nevertheless, it wasn't solely the alterations in surroundings that influenced me; it was also the traumatic situations that arose from living in a country ravaged by war.

Yes, I went through that too…

Witnessing dead bodies on the street, helping a wounded man, and coming across unattended corpses are some of the disturbing visuals that have been ingrained in my mind from a young age.

I witnessed everything. I saw it all. The deaths. The tragedies. The bloodshed. Of course, no such sight can easily be forgotten by any youngster.

I had recurring nightmares after going through these disturbing instances, which resulted in insomnia. At times, I could not sleep for weeks and sometimes even months, replaying those horrific scenes in my mind over and over until one day, they stopped. I did not know how they stopped, but they did, and it was a relief.

Later on in my life, I figured out why those images stopped haunting me. My brain had learned to suppress my negative experiences. I was suppressing those memories and visuals into my subconscious, only for them to resurface surprisingly, unknowingly and probably inconveniently at a later stage in my life.

Over time, both consciously and unconsciously, these significant and distressing experiences impacted my mindset, shaping my perspective and the person I was evolving into. It was difficult, and there was no way to escape from it.

In addition to these significant events, the mindset passed down from my parents' predecessors also strongly impacted me. This inheritance passed on from one generation to the next filled me with a combination of fear and anxiety. The anxiety that arose from the limitations woven into our lives from their narratives. It became a part of who I am.

While I had this natural fear within me, there was also a growing sense of perseverance—a resilience handed down to me by the older generations, too, showing me how to endure and adapt to any situation. This combination of caution and courage influenced my attitude toward life and its obstacles.

My early teenage years were characterized by inconsistency. While enjoying amazing experiences like going to the snow mountains every Sunday in winter with my parents (where my brothers skied while I hesitated to join), camping in the mountains in spring, and going to the beach in summer, the shadow of war lingered.

Throughout the brief period of peace, we had the liberty to explore different territories. However, our activities were still constrained by the persistent fear of conflict and the limited territories we were allowed to visit. The fear never went away. We were unconsciously afflicted by uncertainty.

Before the war, before my 10th birthday, the trips to the nearby mountain were the highlight of our year. These trips were eagerly anticipated as soon as the first chill of autumn crept into the air.

As Christmas approached, eagerness filled the air as my older brother, cousins, and I would go on our exciting adventure. Covered in cozy jackets and scarves, we used to start our journey in the soft morning glow.

As we walked along the trail, excitement grew with every stride. The lively colors of autumn filled the forest, with the crunch of fallen leaves enhancing the magical atmosphere. At every twist in the trail, we looked across the horizon for the ideal Christmas tree, tall and proud, with branches just waiting to be decorated with tinsel and lights. It had to be just right.

Finally, after hours of searching, we would spot it: The tree that would become the centerpiece of our holiday celebrations. With shouts of joy, we used to set to work, carefully sawing through the trunk and lowering it to the forest floor.

As we dragged it back home, branches would brush against our faces, and we couldn't help but feel a sense of triumph.

We knew this long-sought tree would symbolize our holiday spirit in the cold winter months ahead.

Once back home, we started decorating our prized tree, lovingly placing each ornament and strand of tinsel.

Christmas morning was the peak of weeks of preparation. As the first light of dawn filtered through the curtains, forming a radiance over the room, excitement bubbled up inside us like a pot on the verge of boiling over.

We scrambled out of bed, eager to see what treasures awaited us beneath the tree. We gathered in the main hall, and our beautifully decorated Christmas tree greeted us, its branches laden with shimmering ornaments and twinkling lights. The air, pregnant with the scent of pine and cinnamon, wrapped us in a cocoon of holiday magic.

As we gathered around the twinkling branches while exchanging gifts and laughter, we knew our mountain adventures had given us memories that would last a lifetime.

With impatient hands, we would unwrap our gifts, each a token of love and affection from family and friends. The room echoed with laughter and screams of delight as we discovered the prizes hidden beneath layers of wrapping paper.

But more than the gifts, the joy of being together made that morning special. We sat around the tree, sipping hot cocoa, feeling the unmistakable warmth of love in the room. We all knew that our mountain adventures had given us a connection that would withstand anything and everything. We were that sure.

Before Christmas came, with all the holiday love and festivities, there was Halloween.

Halloween was a time of year that sparked our imaginations and filled us with excitement. For our families, it was way more than just dressing up and getting candy; it was a chance to set our creativity free, become someone else for a night, and delight in the thrill of trick-or-treating through the neighborhood.

Weeks ahead of the main evening, we would carefully consider different costume concepts, brainstorming ways to change our appearance into witches, superheroes, or creatures of the dark.

On Halloween night, after ringing a doorbell, we would excitedly say "trick or treat" while holding our bags open to get candy. Wearing masks to conceal our faces and clothes to hide our identities, we reveled in the liberty to embody any persona we desired. It was an opportunity to enter a new world, to be someone or something else for a night.

While going from one house to another, we felt a sense of friendship as the streets were filled with laughter and conversation from other trick-or-treaters.

My connection with my older brother was more than just being siblings; we were like partners in crime, experiencing the ups and downs of childhood together and creating lasting bonds that would stand the test of time.

On the other hand, my little brother was like my own son. I was only 7 years old when he was born, and I cared for him by feeding him and changing his diaper like a grown-up would do. I suppose my mother felt overwhelmed with caring for four children, so she asked me to assist with household tasks and take care of my youngest siblings. Taking care of and providing food for someone else at 7 years old set the groundwork for me to become a mother. Our connection is indestructible, resembling that of a mother and child, as I continue to care for him like he is my own son, justifying his actions and behavior.

There was also my sister, 3 years younger than me, and I babysat her too. She was an active child, and we were always playing and dancing. I was the elder sister at school and was always called to the office to hear the complaints about her and to pass on the message to my mother from the school's management. Our relationship is based on mutual and unconditional love, and we used to wear each other's clothes and accessories as teenagers and adults, as all sisters do.

The involvement of our cousins in our activities strengthened our familial ties, creating memories that would shape our identities. Our cousins were our closest confidants and our companions through every adventure life sent our way.

From the moment we were old enough to toddle around, we formed a strong bond that transcended blood ties. Whether we were exploring the outdoors, creating make-believe worlds, or simply lounging around to swap stories, our cousins were always there, ready to laugh with us, cry with us, and everything in between.

Including our cousins in our activities wasn't just a matter of convenience; it was a conscious choice as a family. We forged memories that would become the cornerstone of our identity, shaping who we were and who we would become in the future. And though time and distance may have separated us physically, the ties we formed with our cousins remain solid.

Television in our household was a form of entertainment; we connected through it to our neighbors and loved ones like moths to a flame. These gatherings at our house weren't just about watching TV; they were opportunities to come together and share stories in each other's company. It wasn't simply about tuning into the latest shows or catching up on the day's news (for adults). Neighbors would drop by, their faces blazing with anticipation as they settled into comfortable chairs and couches, eager to partake, given the black and white screen at that time.

As we giggled, wept, and gasped in unity, we felt a sense of belonging, knowing our home was where friendships were. Those were such pure, soft-hearted times.

For me, having purity and innocence in childhood is important. This is mainly because it represents a period of transparency and naivety, free from the world's complexities. It allows us to perceive life with unspoiled eyes, nurturing openness and curiosity. Emotionally, innocence provides a sense of safety by shielding individuals from the darker parts of reality.

There were many traditions that we, as a family, endowed. Another tradition of collecting snails wasn't just a duty; it was a link to our generations bygone, a nod to our ancestors. For this, we set out after rain showers with baskets, cleaning gardens and shrubs for these slippery treasures. Guided by the wisdom passed down through the ages, we learned the art of patience, savoring the thrill of each discovery. Back home, after collection, we marveled at the intricate beauty of these tiny creatures, all of us gaping at nature's wonders for us.

For the little girl in me, childhood wasn't a time for play; it was a grand exploration where every corner held new wonders. Each moment was magical, from chasing fireflies on summer evenings to building forts in the backyard to being mesmerized by gazing at the starry skies in the summer.

Even during times of sorrow, our family and community served as anchors, offering ease, support, and company. We shared around the dinner table, the love enveloping us like a blanket as we expressed feelings in each other's company. This further united us.

Growing up with my father in Lebanon was an adventure unlike any other. While our peers were content with familiar surroundings, we explored the unknown sides of Lebanon's culture and history.

My parents, especially my father, exemplified a spirit of infectious sociability. They thrived in the company of others, enjoying the opportunity to connect with friends and strangers. Whether attending lively gatherings or hosting functions at home, my parents welcomed everyone with open arms, creating a warm and inviting atmosphere that drew people to them.

In many ways, my childhood was filled with laughter. Yet, beneath the surface lurked the war, spells of fear and uncertainty over our lives. The recurrences of the conflict rang through our streets, reminding us of the fragility of life and the harsh realities of our world. But, despite this fear imposed by war, my parents remained committed in their determination to provide us with normality and security. Their softness in adversity became our hope, guiding us throughout this wartime.

Reflecting on the past, I hold dear the time spent in Lebanon, where family and community were the day's highlight. My early years were a mix of joy and sorrow, achievements and challenges, yet primarily influenced by love and strong family connections.

You can see that, like every human, my childhood laid the groundwork for my entire life. In the security of our surroundings, my siblings and I were able to thrive, supported by the love that enveloped every aspect of our lives. It was a simple childhood but abundant in important treasures like love, unity, and lasting memories.

My father was frequently compared to a brave superhero amidst the chaos of war-ravaged Lebanon. He had a strong presence and showed bravery, leading to many awards for his courageous acts. His energetic presence was noticeable in every corner of the community.

Despite being a traditional homemaker, my mother had an equally vibrant zest for life. My mother is a resilient woman who raised us mostly by herself. As I think about her position as the center of our home, I am constantly stunned by her abilities, particularly because she did not have a formal education. Even though she only received basic instruction in reading and writing, she can manage a household and understand family dynamics effectively.

Now in her late 70s, my mother remains the pillar of our home. Despite having a housekeeper to help with the cleaning, she insists on handling the cooking herself, a task she cherishes passionately. Her dedication to this role highlights her love for her family and her desire to maintain a sense of independence and personal contribution. Till now, her kitchen remains her domain, where she continues to express her care and love through the meals she prepares for herself and my father and myself, my children, and siblings whenever we visit them.

As I previously stated, my parents loved being social, and they often celebrated on weekends with friends, danced, drank, and enjoyed fine food. The affection for being social wasn't limited to only them; it appeared to have been inherited by me and my siblings.

Returning to our residence in central Beirut during and after the war, our house was always bustling with activity. At daybreak, the front door opened, inviting a constant flow of people needing my father's advice or help. Known for his willingness and ability to assist, our home was seldom peaceful. Privacy was hard to come by, and our rest was frequently disturbed by unexpected visitors we couldn't imagine turning away without offering them a meal.

During my teenage years, I would occasionally feel overloaded by spontaneous get-togethers and, at times, would be frustrated by the unexpected disruption of our family routine.

Life was a mixture of simplicity and joy, with its unpredictable pace. My days were brimming with the adventures that only a child's creativity can conjure. I was unaware that significant changes were approaching rapidly beneath the surface of my happy childhood.

EXERCISE

Keep writing and journaling in your nice notebook from the last exercise. Inventory the positive things you remember about your childhood up to age 10.

Describe your childhood home. Include details about your room, your parents, your brothers and sisters, and the environment of your house.

Next, on a new page, jot down all the unpleasant memories from that same period up to the age of 10, and include as much information as possible.

Then, connect the bad memories and negative experiences you went through during that stage of your life to their impact on your teenage life and adulthood.

This exercise will help you understand why you behave in certain ways and the values that make you make certain life decisions. All these decision-making patterns and values are formed by your programming/upbringing and your essence and life purpose.

TESIMONIALS

"Through Jocelyne, I found relief from my physical ailments and a deeper sense of peace that has transformed my life. Her approach to healing goes beyond the physical, touching the soul to one's own healing power. I am grateful for her help, which has brought me to a life of health."

LESSON 2

Cherish every moment of your life and enjoy the present, as we never know what life will bring. No matter where we live, life is constantly changing, and being able to adapt is essential.

Moving to a new city, switching schools, or finding yourself in a new culture takes more than physical adjustments. It would help to be mentally strong to handle life's twists and turns.

Every major change or relocation offers a chance for learning and new beginnings. New starts are gateways to new experiences and connections that help us better understand ourselves and the world around us.

These experiences teach us that we have the power to shape our own story. Each new chapter of our lives is a fresh start and a chance to redefine our journey. If used correctly, the excitement of the unknown brings us adrenaline, driving us farther in life.

We leave behind past mistakes with each new beginning and learn from our new and old experiences. That is the only way to break free from our fears and doubts that weigh us down.

So, with this pen in your hand, you are writing a new chapter of your life with passion, knowing your masterpiece is still unfolding and the best is yet to come.

CHAPTER 3

Wars

Our everyday wholesome routines started to deteriorate when the political atmosphere transitioned from faint background noise to loud banging that could not be ignored.

This was a time when the world appeared to come to a halt and take a deep breath. As the city was engulfed by chaos, the nights turned into intense battles. The soothing blanket turned into a worrisome refuge while the sounds of gunfire and explosions were hell-bent on destroying any chance of peace and calm.

This haunting lullaby of chaos was the background to our nights in those times. It was a reminder that a disaster waiting to happen is lurking right outside our vulnerable home.

Sleep had become a struggle. While in bed, hearing the sounds of war through the thin walls, I would shut my eyes and attempt to picture a place away from the chaos.

Every night, while the noises of war loomed over us, we held fast to the belief that this, too, shall pass.

Day after day, our conversations at bedtime became quieter and quieter against the apocalyptic background of our reality.

Our devastation and helplessness amplified when we heard that our school was closed until further notice. Armed guards replaced the familiar faces of teachers at the gates, and the classrooms, which were once alive with the chatter of students and the scurry of chalk on blackboards, went empty and silent.

These instances, these scenarios, were the omens of the storm that was headed our way. These were the unmistakable signs of a reality we hoped to avoid.

The civil war began on April 13th, 1975, in Beirut. However, in January 1976, two months before my 10th birthday, our lives changed forever.

Our parents, who had always been our leaders of strength, now wore expressions of worry and terror that no assurances could chase away. Conversations at dinner were no longer about our days but about survival, about plans whispered in soft tones and about whether to stay or to flee.

Then, one night, the decisive moment came without any warning.

The kids were lying down under the blankets, trying to block out the bad energy from the violence outside, while adults were talking in hush tones, discussing their survival, when all of a sudden, the sharp, piercing noise of a stray bullet plunging the living room wall rattled us all.

The metal wedged in the plaster was an unquestionable sign that the fragile bubble of safety we had clung to had been broken, and the home that had harbored generations of laughter, love, and memories would soon be left behind, becoming another casualty of the war that mercilessly tore our lives apart.

The Damour massacre took place on 20th January 1976 during the Lebanese Civil War. Our home and birthplace were under a severe attack.

The tensions that had been simmering beneath the surface of our daily life suddenly erupted, transforming the familiar streets of our neighborhood into a land unrecognizable even to those who had spent their entire lives there.

The leading political party in opposition at the time had laid siege to our area, and by the time we were about to leave, our city was taken over by forces that viewed everyone through the prism of religious sects.

That night, we huddled together for some time. We knew we were leaving what was most precious to us — our family and Home. Within hours, we were forced to make unimaginable decisions about what to take and leave behind.

With trembling hands and hearts heavy with grief, we packed a single carry-on bag. We couldn't carry anything except our precious belongings, documents and clothes. Cash and jewelry, tangible assets that might provide security in the uncertain days ahead, were kept in our bags.

Essential documents like birth certificates and identification papers were tucked between layers of clothing. Each item we decided to keep with us carried a weight of presence.

The clothes we wore that night felt foreign on our bodies as if putting them on; we were stepping into the roles of refugees, roles we had never imagined we would play.

A sense of loss enveloped us as we locked the door to our home for the last time. My father's hand hesitated on the key for a moment longer than necessary. The click of the lock echoed. It was a sound marking the end of an era.

At that time, I glanced around the neighborhood. Each corner was filled with tears and countless moments of my childhood. But I knew we had to go now.

We turned our backs on the door, on the life we had known, and my father took a deep breath. In a voice that carried the bulk of our determination, he said, "Let's go. A new journey awaits us."

With those words, we stepped into the darkness of the unknown, leaving behind the past. The roads led us away from everything we had known and loved. This ride into the nameless was marked by moments of reflection. Each glance back at the disappearing outline of our home was a stab of realization about the gravity of our situation.

My family and I were to join a stream of others seeking safety like us. People were already gathered at the Saadiyat castle of Lebanon's former president, 6 kilometers from our home. From there, we were supposed to be flown by helicopter to a nearby city called 'Deir al Amar.'

I remember how, on our way to 'Saadiyat,' the car's headlights pierced the dimness, which seemed to dance scarily around us. Every turn, every alley we passed, felt fraught with danger. The silence within the car was loud. It was as if we held our breath, hoping our vehicle would become invisible to the surrounding mayhem.

My younger siblings, too young to fully comprehend the situation, slept restlessly in the backseat.

"Stay down," my father instructed softly as we approached a checkpoint. The tension in the car increased up another notch, and I crouched lower, my eyes squeezed shut. I could hear the sounds of the night outside filtering in—a barking dog, the rumble of an engine, and gunfire.

We cleared the checkpoint after verification, and under the cloak of night, we managed to join the mass departure of those seeking safety away from the frontlines.

Meanwhile, the civil war in Lebanon was not a conflict confined to the battlefields. The distinctions between fighters and civilians became increasingly obscured as the war entered daily existence.

The beautiful and vibrant city of Beirut was not the same anymore. Neighborhoods that had been scenes of harmony had transformed into contested zones, where allegiances shifted like the sand, and the specter of violence was always present.

In Beirut, the distinction between East and West became a symbol of the nation's fractured identity, with checkpoints replacing crosswalks and snipers dictating the flow of life. The Green Line, a no-man's land that bisected the capital, stood as a glaring cue of the divisions that had taken root, turning city blocks into warzones and apartment buildings into ramparts.

Once removed from the political planning of urban centers, rural villages found themselves unwilling hosts to militias and foreign armies. Fields where crops once grew became staging grounds for military operations, with farmers caught in the crossfire, their livelihoods sacrificed to strategic objectives they had little part in deciding. The agricultural life was disrupted by the demands of war, forcing families to abandon their homes and businesses to seek safety in places already overwhelmed by the influx of people.

Even religious institutions were not immune to the conflict's reach. Churches and mosques, which had served as gathering points, found themselves on the front lines, their summits and minarets bearing witness to the violence. The sanctity of these places was violated by the war, turning spaces of worship into shelters and, in some tragic instances, targets.

The war's bearing on the society of Lebanon was deep, forcing individuals to direct a setting where the lines between friend and foe, welfare and danger constantly shifted. Families were torn apart. The war demanded choices that pitted neighbor against neighbor, brother against brother, in a struggle for survival.

The simple act of volunteering outside for bread or water became a dangerous task. Families were banished, their homes destroyed or abandoned in the desperate search.

Groups had to unite in solidarity, offering shelter and support to those most affected by the conflict. Acts of kindness and humanity, small yet significant, became the only hope. These gestures, often overlooked in the account of the war, spoke to the spirit of the Lebanese people.

After leaving our home and clearing checkpoints, we reached the "Saadiyat" castle at the sea, where families hugged each other with lines of worry carved into their brows. Parents held their children close, whispering words of comfort that contradicted the worry in their eyes.

They created protective circles around the youngest among us, their bodies shielding the children from the harsh escape. The children, for their part, looked around with wide eyes, their usual liveliness dimmed by the unfamiliar surroundings and the tense atmosphere.

Individuals who had set out alone, leaving behind their families to forge a path to safety for them to follow, bore the unmistakable quality of strong character. Their gazes stood fixed on the horizon as a silent pledge to themselves to overcome the tricky ride and somehow reunite with their loved ones in a safe place.

That night, we slept on the floor, at the garage of the castle, together with hundreds of families like us. My father discussed the situation with the country's ex-president and other leaders inside the castle.

It turned out that 'Deir al Amar' and the paths toward the area were unsafe for us after some sudden changes happened within the opposing party and their new passageways. With all routes locked, we found ourselves trapped, with the sea as our only option to escape.

The following morning, my father sent my cousin to tell us that he would arrange for us to leave by sea at any moment today.

My mom instructed my siblings and me to stay where we were and that she would go and be right back. Being obedient, I stayed back while my siblings ran after her. My mom turned around, grabbed my younger siblings' hands and walked out with my eldest brother in her tow. Before leaving, she instructed me, "Don't move, keep the bag with you, don't go anywhere and don't leave the bag till I come back."

How could she trust a barely 10-year-old to keep guard of jewelry, valuables, and so much cash?

How could she put such a burden and responsibility on a kid?

My mother and siblings were gone for hours, and I waited alone, surrounded by strangers, sitting on the bare floor during winter. Then, finally, in the late afternoon, she returned with my siblings, took the bag, which was heavy for me to carry, and off we went to the shore from where we were supposed to depart.

We stood on the rocks on the shore, waiting and waiting, unsure of what was happening. Around us, people were shouting, yelling, and fighting over who would board the small boats first. These small boats were taking people from the rocks to the cargo ship, preparing to return for more passengers.

It was winter, and the daylight faded quickly, making it cold and dark earlier than usual. We soon jumped on one of the small boats, which took us to that same cargo ship, which was a few kilometers in the waters as it could not dock near the rocks.

My mom argued with my dad since he told her he would stay behind. He promised to follow us in a few days, but my mom did not have any of it. She was screaming and shouting that we wouldn't go without him. And finally, he agreed to jump in with us to drop us to the ship.

Now, you must know that this boat was a humble vessel. A small space of desperation, overcrowded beyond its means. It swayed with the weight of too many souls for its size. The boat meant for 5 people was carrying ten people. Ten souls:

My parents, my three siblings, myself, three of our cousins and the boatman, each with a story of their own.

It was just before dark when we got on that small boat, and we could see the fire and smoke rising from our beloved Damour. Each of us felt helpless as we watched our city turn into ashes.

Even though the boat had no personal space, a sense of solidarity bound us.

The actions of those around us intensely depicted the undying human spirit while facing misfortune. Moments of silence spoke of the grief for what was lost.

As we floated further away from the land we called home, the overcrowded boat protected us and our families.

The weight of ten souls was pressing down not just with the heft of our bodies but with the emotional burdens we carried. The heavy coats everyone wore weren't just layers against the biting cold of January; they were armor, as if thick wool and fabric could shield us from more than the wind. Each coat bore the weight of silent fears, of thoughts unspoken but shared, filling the air like a fog that refused to lift.

The fear gripped our chests, tightening with each uncertain glance at the rough sea.

We were relieved to be saved from death and sad to leave our home and city, but mostly, we were afraid of the sea and the unknown that awaited us.

As we were about to reach the cargo ship, our worst fears came true.

Our little boat got filled with seawater, which led the boat to flip upside down. In the breathless seconds that followed, time seemed to suspend in a collective gasp held in the chests of every passenger as we faced the sudden misfortune.

The sudden catastrophe plunged us all into the freezing waters. Panic and terror gripped us as we fought for our lives. The water prepared to fill our lungs as the cold seeped into our bones.

We observed the sea claiming everything in its path. People, possessions, hopes—all were engulfed in the icy waters that closed over us. The shock of the coldness was like a thousand needles piercing the skin, a welcome by the unforgiving sea.

Our warm coats, now heavy and freezing with water, were pulling us down. Gasps for air were cut short by waves that rolled over us, one after another, relentless in their assault. The darkness of the night compounded the terror, transforming the water into a void where up and down lost all meaning.

Survival instincts took over—flailing limbs fought against the pull of the deep sea, desperate for a lifeline, for a breath.

My family and our cousins reached out to each other in the darkness, finding one another through instinct.

"Over here!" I heard someone shout, their voice hoarse with fear.

We followed each other frantically, paddling toward another small boat sent to rescue us and then taken towards the huge cargo ship.

We all found ways to get out of the water by any and every means.

"Everyone's going to be alright now," one of the soldiers said as I was pulled up on the deck.

This hour-long, terrifying, and transformative experience underscored a truth that would echo throughout my life: "Within us lies an incredible capacity to overcome adversity and adapt."

That night, the universe was testing our endurance. We faced different challenges once aboard the cargo ship that offered us all refuge.

The cold, biting air clung to our skin, with wet clothes sticking stubbornly to our trembling bodies.

We immediately removed the icy clothes and wrapped ourselves in the provided blankets. We all were coping with the immediate physical discomfort and the more unsettling realization of our dangerous situation and the mental stress that came with it.

The dirty and unkempt ship was far from the safety we hoped for. Yet, aboard this vessel, we made our way to a new city, where probable safety awaited us.

"We'll make it through," my father's voice soothed my soul as an anchor in the sea of terrors. "We are safe. That's what matters now", he added.

While we clung to the hope around us, the sounds of sobbing, whispered prayers, and the occasional comforting words exchanged between passengers filled the space. A crew member, his face tired but not unkind, approached us. "Try to rest," he suggested, hinting at the demanding journey ahead. He was right; we did not know what to expect after getting off this ship.

After a few hours, we got off the ship, and the city that loomed before me was unfamiliar. It was a maze of streets with faces of refugees everywhere.

In this moment of overwhelming disorientation, a family friend my father had known for years through bonds of mutual respect stepped forward to greet us. His face was scraped with the same lines of worry and fatigue that mirrored my father's. Seeing us, he broke into a smile of recognition and relief.

"Welcome," he said, his voice warmly contrasting the cold since our departure.

"You'll stay with me. I have a place for you," he added. His offer was a reminder that despite the upheaval and loss, humanity and kindness still existed.

He led us through the city and took us to an apartment. He was living in a new villa he had built for himself and his family, and luckily, no one lived there.

It was furnished modestly, yet every piece of furniture, every draping curtain, felt like a luxury compared to the dire conditions we had endured.

"This is your home now," our angel said as he opened the door, gesturing us inside with a sweeping motion. "It's not much, but it's safe and yours for as long as you need."

The ease that washed over us is indescribable. We collectively sighed in relief as we stepped into our new home.

With sadness brimming in his eyes, my father reached out to him and held his hands in a silent expression of gratitude that no words could satisfactorily convey. "Thank you," he whispered, his voice choked with tears. "You've given us more than a shelter; you've given us…everything."

Our host nodded with humility. "We take care of our own," he replied.

This new stability, though comforting, could not fully erase the harrowing experiences that preceded it.

Nightmares frequently shattered the quiet of the night with intense replays of our time adrift at sea—the cold water enclosing me and the fear of never seeing the light of day kept me awake.

Each morning, I woke up with the blurred lines between reality and memory, with the remnants of that night's terrors still clinging to my consciousness like cobwebs in the corners of my mind.

In this stillness, I traced the contours of my memories, piecing together fragments of a happier past that felt increasingly distant with each passing day. The laughter of childhood echoed in the recesses of my mind, a bittersweet strain that mingled with loss and longing.

I mourned what was gone. Yet, I somehow found myself clinging to the flickering flame of hope that refused to be extinguished. Of course, it was fragile and a fleeting spark, but it burned with a fierceness that defied my gloom.

This relocation to "Jounieh" marked a drastic change from the life I had known, yet it offered a fragment of normalcy amid the disarray that had become my reality.

EXERCISE

The negative experiences you had as a child have created a link between your current circumstances and the essence of those experiences. These patterns keep repeating, often with different people, locations, and circumstances, but the emotions and attitudes remain the same.

These patterns must be broken to turn your life around and make significant changes.

So, how do you break these patterns?

Write them in your notebook and address them.

Becoming self-aware and recognizing these patterns is half the work, and forgiving the people who caused the pain and these bad experiences is the key to your healing process.

So for this exercise, as an example, you should first write: I forgive you, mom or dad, uncle or grandparent or any person who caused you harm or pain, followed by how they caused you pain and the feelings and emotions resulting from these experiences.

Second, you write: I forgive myself for allowing you, mom, dad, uncle etc… to cause me pain…

And in the third part, you write: Mom, dad, uncle etc... please forgive me for whatever I made you feel.

You keep repeating this exercise until you feel you have forgiven the people.

Every few days, return to your notebook and write these forgiveness notes. You will start remembering other people to forgive and other emotions and feelings.

Acknowledging these people and feelings and forgiving them is a cornerstone in your healing. Enjoy this exercise because as much as it is painful, it is rewarding, but only if you keep repeating it religiously.

One day, there will be no one left to forgive and no bad childhood experiences to acknowledge, and you will be relieved of your burdens and patterns that weigh you down.

I forgave those who destroyed our home, our childhood belongings, our city, and our country… and I am compassionate towards them and those who face similar situations, whether they are victims or the perpetrators, as both victims and abusers are going through their own journeys and pain.

TESTIMONIALS

"Our teenager was on the brink of dropping out of school in his 11th grade, completely dissatisfied with his education. After a few months of working with Jocelyne, his outlook completely transformed. He not only finished high school but is now successful in his second year of university. We are thankful for helping our son see his potential and guiding him through a crucial phase of his life."

LESSON 3

I used to hold onto the past, clinging to old hurts and doubts. It felt safe and familiar, even if it was drowning me. But one day, I realized I was missing out on the beauty of today, caught in a storm of what-ifs and could-haves.

Letting go of what I knew wasn't easy. It felt like tearing off a protective layer, exposing my raw emotions. But with each layer I shed, I discovered a strength I never knew I had. It was like shedding heavy chains and finally being able to breathe freely.

I began to see that my past, while painful, had also made me resilient. With all my quirks and scars, it shaped me into the person I am today. They are a part of my story.

I started to trust that life has a plan, even when it feels chaotic. There's a bigger picture I can't always see, but I started learning to surrender to it. It's like letting go of the steering wheel and trusting the universe to guide me.

It's scary, I won't lie. But with each step forward, I felt a sense of peace and purpose. I'm still discovering new passions and building deeper connections with the universe.

Indeed, life is a journey, not a destination, and right now, I'm enjoying the ride.

CHAPTER 4

From Scratch

We stayed at the apartment my father's friend offered us on our arrival to Jounieh for a week and then moved to a bigger place in the same city.

As time passed and weeks turned into months, we started to reconstruct our lives. It was a slow journey marked by obstacles, challenges, instances of luck, and moments of unexpected joy.

I found comfort in the daily routine of life - in the smell of food cooking in our kitchen, the sound of children playing outside, and the friendship of our new neighbors.

Gradually, the wounds caused by the war started to heal, and we stepped into the beginning of a fresh start in a new city.

We gradually began to construct a resemblance of daily existence in Jounieh by starting school even though it was close to the end of the academic year.

Jounieh was a beautiful city in the Keserwan District. It was located on the seaside, just 16 kilometers north of Beirut. As we adjusted to this bustling city famous for its beautiful coast and vibrant entertainment scene, we felt great returning to our routines. It seemed like everything was going to be okay.

The peaceful scenery of the city, featuring stunning vistas of the Mediterranean Sea and the verdant mountains around, provided a calming change from our recent struggles.

In its history, Jounieh was a peaceful fishing town but had now become a bustling activity center. The lively pathway, adorned with palm trees, extended along the shoreline, providing a perfect route for evening walks as the sun went down.

Jounieh was abuzz with numerous festivals and cultural events that attract locals and tourists all year round. The main attraction to this day is the Festival of Jounieh, a vibrant summer event filled with fireworks, music performances, and processions, bringing a festive atmosphere to the city.

The summers were the highlight of life in Jounieh city. We arrived in Jounieh in January, and after four months of living there, the beach season started.

The end of May and the beginning of June are the times we all wait to enjoy the warmth of the sun and the long days as the sun sets late.

As summer's heat enveloped the coastline in its golden light, I returned to the sea again, eager to bask in the sun's warmth.

Despite the joyful atmosphere, the memory of our small boat turning upside down while our heavy, soaked clothes pulled us down toward imminent death manifested as a fear of water whenever I was close to the beach.

The fear of drowning kept me from enjoying swimming, which once was my ultimate pleasure. With each playful splash and swell of laughter, I teetered between fear and courage, unsure whether to fully surrender to the sea or stay back. I longed to lose myself in the waves, but there remained a lingering reluctance that held me back.

My eldest brother, three years older than me, was always there to encourage and help me. He would gently say, "I'll hold your hand. Nothing will happen." We repeated this process many times, and his reassuring presence helped me build confidence each time. We kept this up until. Eventually, I returned to the water and started to swim without fear again.

With his constant support, my hesitance gradually faded away and slowly but surely, I let go of my fears and allowed myself to be swept away by the sea.

I realized something important in those moments: Sometimes, the most significant moments are the courage to decide.

My brother's unwavering support helped me rediscover the joy and freedom of swimming, transforming my fear into one of the best experiences of my life.

Later on in life, to my delight, my daughter became good at swimming. Part of my children's curriculum was swimming lessons for one semester. Her PE teacher quickly noticed her talent and chose her to represent the school in a competition with other local schools.

When her teacher said, "We would like your daughter to represent the school in the upcoming swim competition," I felt an overwhelming sense of pride.

As the competition approached, I watched her practice with dedication and enthusiasm. "Mom, I can't wait for the competition," she said, her eyes excitedly shining.

Her success in the competition felt like a tremendous victory and an achievement, not just for her but for me.

"You did it!" I exclaimed, hugging her tightly after she won her race. Her accomplishment had a special meaning, given everything I had experienced and overcome in the past. It was as if her win symbolized the winning over of my fear.

Watching her excel brought a deep sense of pride and fulfillment. "I'm so proud of you," I told her with tears in my eyes.

"You achieved something I once struggled with, "I said.

Her achievement reminded me of the courage it took me to face my fears after what happened the night our boat flipped when we were escaping Beirut. Seeing her swim and win made me even more proud.

I was terrified to get back in the water after the Beirut incident but with the help of my brother, my fear of the sea subsided after the magical summer in Jounieh. After almost a year and a half—just as I was getting used to the new city, school system, the teachers, making new friends, enjoying the beach, and becoming familiar with the neighborhood—we moved again.

Moving again felt weird. After all that we went through, I thought Jounieh was the place where we were going to start fresh but that was not the case and we had to move.

This time, our destination was "Achrafieh," a central area back in Beirut, and once we moved, I gradually lost touch with those I had met in Jounieh.

Achrafieh, one of Beirut's oldest and most charming districts, became our new home. Situated in the city's eastern part, Achrafieh is a montage of culture and modernity, characterized by its blend of historical architecture and contemporary lifestyle. This area, known for its narrow, winding streets and beautiful, old French Mandate-era buildings, projects sophistication and timeless elegance.

As we settled into Achrafieh, I realized that the hustle and bustle of this densely populated place were different from the more laid-back seaside vibe of Jounieh.

Achrafieh's streets were lined with various shops, cafes, and eateries that served everything from traditional Lebanese dishes to international cuisines. The area was also a cultural center, home to several art galleries, boutiques, and antique stores, offering a sight into the past and present Lebanese artistry.

We enrolled in a new school again, which became my 4th school. In Damour, I attended two different schools. One was within walking distance from our house, where I went from kindergarten to grade one. The second was a bit farther, in a different district of Damour, and we took the school bus to get there. After that, I attended a school in Jounieh, and now I was at a fourth school—and I hadn't even turned 12 yet.

By then, adaptation had become my new hobby, so I adjusted to our new surroundings and made new friends. This came with its own set of contests and opportunities. The schools here are often prestigious institutions with a rigorous academic environment and a strong emphasis on extracurricular activities. This gave my siblings and me a chance to receive an education while immersing ourselves in a bubbling pot of ideas and the diverse demographic that Achrafieh attracted.

My parents still live in our home in Achrafieh. It ended up becoming our permanent residence amid the ongoing commotion.

During the entire ordeal, our ability to bounce back from adversity was consistently put to the test. The effects of the initial conflict had already influenced our day-to-day existence, turning our neighbors from strangers into a vast support system that was like a family to us.

Throughout that period, my father was driven by his obligation to serve in combat, and because of that, he was frequently away from our everyday routines for long periods. Only the four of us were with our mother, and we were completely unaware of our father's arrival or departure schedule.

During the escalation of the Lebanese Civil War, the events of 1982 had a lasting impact on us. Misfortune and violence were still lingering in our backyard.

Attacks, blasts, and infiltrations caused extensive destruction, extending to the core of our neighborhoods and interrupting the delicate peace we sometimes achieved.

In that same year, the murder of the newly elected Lebanese president in Achrafieh, a terrifying incident that occurred in our neighborhood, caused great fear in our lives. Beirut's streets transformed into hazardous pathways with imminent threats of danger looming. Our daily life was filled with the sound of occasional bombings and occasional explosions. Every detonation created a severe sense of uncertainty around us, with each boom resonating in the streets and vibrating in our chests.

Between the brief breaks of peace, the city would quickly rejuvenate as if it had eagerly awaited peace. Markets opened, and children played in the streets again, only to be forced back inside by the next surge of violence.

All of this left us all very puzzled. Residing in this enduring state of fear from violence was a challenge that pushed our resilience to its limits. Unexpected interruptions became a regular occurrence in our lives, with schools shutting down without warning, events ending abruptly, and the constant need to reassure scared children as the night sky was illuminated not by stars but by the glare of fire.

The dream of lasting peace seemed far-fetched in Beirut, a city trapped by its physical location and the region's politics.

During the harsh reality of war, my thoughts frequently drifted to my early days in Damour, where the joy of simple pleasures faded.

EXERCISE

Make a list!

List: Worry, fear, anger, sadness, and trying too hard.

Write these next to each other, and write how intense these feelings are for you and how much they affect your daily decisions.

Write 'worry,' and you can describe the feeling next to it.

For example:

Worry: I don't take a taxi because I am worried that the car is dirty and I might catch a virus or get sick.

Fear: I don't leave the house before I double- and triple-check if I have switched off all the lights, checked the gas cooker, closed the windows fully, switched off all electronics, etc.

Write a description for every one of the 5 attitudes as much as you can.

This exercise will help you understand yourself and your fears and doubts and identify the areas and aspects of your life that you must work on and heal from. Doing this will give you clarity, which will be the seed of your healing.

TESTIMONIALS

"I was suicidal. When I started sessions with Jocelyne, I was depressed. But, her effective approach helped me turn my life around in just a few months. I've since moved to a new job, received promotions, and improved my overall life quality. I can't thank her enough for her guidance and for believing in me when I needed it the most. Jocelyne is not only my healer; she is my idol!"

LESSON 4

Adapt to what life throws at you, and thrive on learning the lessons the universe teaches you. Learning, moving forward, and enjoying the changes will be the driving forces behind the desired change you are bringing into your life.

Life is a journey full of twists and turns, with constant changes and unexpected events popping up along the way. From personal loss to career setbacks and all the unforeseen bumps in the road, we all face moments that demand us to adapt.

The real magic happens when we learn from these experiences and find joy in the transformation.

Adaptation isn't just about reacting to what life throws at us. It's about proactively recognizing when things need to change and adjusting our mindset accordingly. Think about technology, for instance. In a constantly evolving world, sticking to old ways can leave us behind, while adapting to new technologies can open doors to exciting opportunities.

The same goes for personal challenges. Facing adversity means acknowledging the need to adapt—whether picking up new skills, shifting our perspective, or changing how we approach a problem. Adapting to change involves dealing with immediate issues and learning valuable lessons from those experiences.

Every challenge holds a chance for growth and self-improvement. Reflecting on what happened, what worked, and what didn't can help us avoid making the same mistakes and make better decisions in the future.

Take someone who loses their job, for example. It's tough but also an opportunity to rethink career goals, gain new skills, and explore different fields.

Learning from setbacks allows finding new opportunities matching their strengths and interests. Changes often bring new chances for growth and new experiences.

Finding joy during change is all about shifting our perspective. Instead of just focusing on the discomfort of leaving behind the familiar, it's crucial to appreciate the new experiences and opportunities that come with it. Celebrating small victories, recognizing personal growth, and being grateful for the lessons learned can boost our overall well-being and the pace of progress.

You might feel excitement and anxiety if you've started a new business or pursued a new passion. But focusing on the positives, the sense of accomplishment, the thrill of exploring new interests, and the satisfaction of achieving goals can give you unexplainable energy and joy in the journey.

By learning from your experiences, and finding joy in the transformation, you turn challenges into opportunities and become stronger and more fulfilled.

Life's unpredictability reminds us that growth comes from unexpected places and that the change is good.

CHAPTER 5

Circles

Beirut was marked by separation based on religious and sectarian affiliations. The nation was divided, its history characterized by turmoil, while its streets echoed with the continued unrest reflected in the sad remains of buildings destroyed by war and bullets.

My brothers, sister and I returned to school and worked on getting used to the school routine. Every day, when we entered the school gates, we found ourselves in a world that tried to uphold a sense of normalcy.

Classrooms provided us with stability and opportunity to learn, but we knew something could go wrong.

Teachers and students attempted to concentrate on class discussions, assignments, and tests despite facing the lasting impact of war. Balancing education and dealing with the consequences of conflict was a challenge.

In this educational environment, we focused on academic subjects while gaining insights into the values of determination, optimism, and unity as a community. Our teachers' lectures were filled with a noticeable wave of inspiration, leadership, and encouragement. It was like they were subtly showing us how to work our way in times of war.

In this setting, young people started to create their paths, gradually putting together the pieces of their disrupted lives as the city worked towards recovery.

The trauma of our escape, particularly the life-threatening scenario at the sea and the loss of our home, had already left deep scars on me.

These two incidents changed my worldview and my approach to life. The fear instilled by the war, the close encounters with death, and the cost of everything we once held dear became a blurry lens through which I viewed the world.

This newfound caution manifested in my personality and, most prominently, in my parenting journey. It increased my tendency to overprotect, which became both a shield and a burden for my children and me.

Every decision I made, from my children's daily activities to their social interactions, was infused with an acute awareness of the dangers and uncertainties that life could present at any time and change everything.

I had seen it happen with my own eyes in the worst ways, so I was constantly vigilant, expecting possible risks and strived to create a cocoon of safety around my children.

While born out of love, this protective instinct carried on with its own weight.

This trauma burdened me with the fear of what could happen if I let my guard down and allowed them to stray too far from the path I considered safe. In my efforts to shield them from harm, I sometimes struggled to balance promoting their independence and ensuring their safety. It was a delicate tightrope that I walked for so long.

One day, my son came to me and said, "Mom, you can't live in fear all the time. You can't live your life being scared of everything I do. We live in Dubai; it's safe here. There's no war here. Please remember that."

I paused and thought about his words. The boy was right.

"You're right," I replied. "I need to work on my own insecurities."

From that moment, I made a conscious effort to change. It wasn't easy, but I took small steps daily to overcome my fears. I gradually felt more at peace, knowing my son was right and we were safe.

Gradually, I understood that real strength is not found in protecting our loved ones from all difficulties but in empowering them to face life's challenges with bravery. As I slowly let go and let them find their way, I found the empowering impact of trust and faith in both them and life's journey.

However, I only came to this realization after many sleepless nights, worrying incessantly, sending constant messages and making phone calls until they returned home and I could finally rest.

The next day, I would feel unsettled due to the impact of sleep deprivation and exhaustion on me, which resulted in me getting frustrated with every error my team made or any problem I had to address at work. It impacted how I felt and my overall health.

As I think about my early experiences, it is evident that the impact of the trauma and fear I went through had a lasting effect on my mind.

In the end, my experience with trauma showed me the significance of recognizing and dealing with the influence it had on my life and the lives of others. By facing my fears and reaching out for help when necessary, I realized that I could start to recover from previous injuries and build a more optimistic, promising future for me and my children.

Realizing that the traumas we experience, particularly during childhood, can have a lasting impact on our behaviors and reactions as adults was thought-provoking.

The fear and trauma I experienced served as both a challenge and a teacher. It molded me and impacted my choices, upbringing, and outlook. However, by reflecting and comprehending, I managed to navigate these challenges and discovered resilience in vulnerability and progress in bravery and optimism.

Despite the persistent presence of violence, there were moments of brightness. For us and many others like us, Beirut has transformed from a mere city to a representation of determination.

Our trips back and forth between Dubai and Achrafieh, where my parents still live in the same apartment we bought many years ago, remind us of our strong ties to the city. Over time, this apartment on a bustling street transformed into our cherished home.

Each return to Beirut is a homecoming, a chance to reconnect with the memories within its walls. Walking through the familiar corridors and gazing at the cityscape below, I feel nostalgic and belonging. In this space, surrounded by my teenage years and adulthood and the warmth of family, I find comfort in the world's chaos.

Coming back to Achrafieh in Beirut after Jounieh, my life became intricately tangled with the city's heartbeat, and as we went from our home city of Beirut to Dubai, the air sizzled with anticipation but also mingled with the bittersweet tang of farewell. It was another significant moment of transition, a crossing of thresholds.

During Our time in Achrafieh, my family sought respite in a beach resort for the summer season of that year.

"Let's try to enjoy some peace," my father said as we arrived at the beach resort with only a few clothes and kitchenware just for the summer. His voice was full of determination and liveliness, but peace was a fleeting luxury.

Little did we know that there were still issues being woven by politicians and their allies that summer. On Monday morning, my father and eldest brother decided to venture into Beirut for necessary errands.

"We'll be back soon," my father assured us as they left, leaving my mother, my younger siblings and me behind at the resort. We had a chalet on the 11th floor of the resort tower. We waved them off, expecting another serene day by the sea.

But just a couple of hours later, as my mom was cooking, my younger siblings were enjoying their swim at the pool, and I was tidying the chalet; the abrupt onset of gunfire shattered the calm.

The terrifying cracks of gunshots replaced the serene sounds of a summer day.

"Get down!" my mother screamed, her voice filled with panic. With only the thin fabric of our swimsuits as armor and bare feet, we found ourselves thrust again into the throes of conflict.

We quickly ran down the stairs, pressing our backs against the walls, knowing from all the experiences we had during the war that we should never use the lifts when there was gunfire.

"Stay close to me," my mother instructed, tightening grip on my hand. She was starting to worry about my younger siblings, as we didn't know what had happened to them. After tidying the chalet, the beach day I planned to enjoy turned into a chaotic scene. The unforgiving reality replaced the serenity we hoped for.

We kept running down the stairs, and the sound of gunfire echoed even louder than with each step we took. We were running towards the main battlefield but did not know that.

When we arrived on the ground floor, we saw the armed men and realized we were in more danger than we had thought.. We did not know who was attacking us. We stayed on the ground floor, by force, for a few hours, and then we were led to the basement when the gunfire stopped.

We sat there for more hours, not allowed to go anywhere—not even to the toilets or to look for my younger siblings. My mom was begging the armed men to find my siblings.

"They probably are on the other side of the resort. There are some people taking refuge in one of the bungalows. Pray that they are there and not dead," an armed man said to my mom.

The shadows of war were never far behind, even in moments when we tried to escape them. Little did we know that day would become a historic day.

The Safra massacre, also known as the Day of the Long Knives, happened in the coastal town of Safra, just north of Beirut, on July 7, 1980. This violent event was part of the

Lebanese Civil War, a complex and brutal conflict that took place from 1975 to 1990.

The Safra massacre was a planned attack orchestrated by the leader of the Phalangist militia, Bachir Gemayel, against the Tigers militia, which Dany Chamoun led.

On that day, heavily armed men attacked the Tigers militia headquarters and several key locations in Safra. They aimed to eliminate the Tigers and their leaders, who they saw as rivals fighting for control over Lebanon's Christian factions.

As a result, many of the Tiger's leaders and members were killed, weakening the faction significantly.

The violence of the Safra massacre did not stay confined to the attack site. It spread to the nearby area, reaching the resort where many families, including my own, had chalets.

Our resort, located only 500 meters from Safra, had its piece of the massacre. This marked a turning point in the power struggle among the Christian Lebanese militias. It also showed the widespread and random nature of the violence during the Lebanese Civil War.

This situation caused civilians, including ourselves, to feel extremely insecure about the unstable condition of the country. However, with the escalation of the conflict, we had no choice but to pass through the warzone that was once a peaceful sanctuary.

Our departure from the resort, led by the fighters during the chaos of the fight, was another harrowing struggle for survival, with the added terror of passing by the fallen bodies.

This experience was a challenging assessment of emotions and minds, completely removing any traces of innocence or ignorance we may have clung to.

Not having any information about my younger siblings' well-being, who were at the pool when the violence started, was extremely painful. We were in disbelief over what had occurred and how closely connected we were as a family. It shook me to the very core of my being.

I vividly recall praying fervently for the safety of my siblings, picturing my sister and brother hiding in fear yet remaining unharmed. The vision was vivid and bright, and I reassured my mom by telling her I had seen it and they were going to be alright.

I told my mom, "I saw them. They're safe."

She looked at me strangely and said, "How do you know that?"

"I just know, Mom. I saw them sitting on the floor in a room. They're safe," I replied, feeling sure but also confused.

At the time, I didn't understand what was happening to me or how I knew. I was only 14 and knew nothing about the gifts the Creator had granted me. But the image was clear in my mind, and it gave me the strength to comfort my mom even though she weirdly looked at me, not knowing what to say.

I did not understand how, but I saw them clearly in a vision. And later on, when my brother told us they were sitting on the floor in a corner, it was exactly the scene I had envisioned.

Only recently did I acknowledge these gifts, and I am grateful for them. As I grew older, I started to notice more moments like that. Sometimes, I would know things or have clear images. It felt strange and even a little scary at times.

One day, I talked to a close friend about it. She told me, "You have a special gift. Not everyone can see things like you do."

Hearing that made me feel better and less alone. I began to read and learn more about intuition and these kinds of gifts. Slowly, I started to trust myself and these feelings more.

Now, I look back and see those moments as blessings. I feel like the Creator gave me these gifts for a reason. They help me make decisions, protect the people I love, and sometimes bring peace in difficult times.

I'm growing, but I'm not scared anymore. I'm thankful for these gifts and the way they guide me. My intuition reminds me that there is something bigger watching over us and that I have a special part to play in this grand play by the cosmic artisan that is our Creator.

Our creator has saved my family and me so many times during the various wars we have witnessed. That day, it was a blessing that my dad and eldest brother left for Beirut. Otherwise, they would have been killed, as the militia were killing any men they saw. They even killed the pool cleaners, among whom was an elderly man. They showed no mercy.

Recalling the visions and intuitive scenarios, another realization unfolded for me: Every time I followed my intuition, I was happy with the results and right all the time. When I often did not follow my intuitions, ignored them, or just dismissed them, not believing in my gut feeling, I was proved wrong and later regretted my decisions.

Looking back, I realize how crucial it is to listen to that inner voice. The voice of your spirit guides your higher self, and intuition is there to guide you to your highest potential.

It's not always easy to trust intuition or gut feeling, especially when others doubt or question your decisions, but I've learned that my intuition is a powerful tool. It has shown me the right path more times than I can count.

Now, I have a grip on it completely, knowing it's a gift that helps me.

Reflecting on these years of survival and finding my gift, it's clear that the major wars and their impacts are not merely historical events but central parts of my personal story.

That was not my last experience with war; I had to endure more, as the circle for me was still incomplete. However, that was the last time I walked over corpses.

That day, I was in a complete fight or flight mode for long hours, starving, scared and not knowing what was happening. Every time we heard gunfire or an explosion, we didn't know if we would die or live to see another day.

The impression of these wars and the years spent during them on my life cannot be overstated. They instilled in me a fear born of necessity but also a determination to protect my loved ones at all costs. It gave me an awareness of the preciousness of life and how to relish it no matter what it throws at us. Through it all, I gained something good—a deep-seated need to find meaning and purpose in everything in life and also ensure that the suffering my family and I faced was not in vain.

EXERCISE

Please write in your notebook/ journal any major incidents or events that happened in your life, how they affected you, how you felt at the time, and the people around those significant events.

Notice if these experiences scarred you or taught you a lesson. Note down if they changed your beliefs or how you view the world.

This inventory will help you know yourself better and help you find and heal your weaknesses.

Once you journal and wish to activate your intuition, hold your wrist with the other hand on the dent below the wrist bone. This will activate and harmonize your intuition; you can use it whenever necessary.

Please note that this is applicable for both males and females. The only difference between them is that men should give this practice more time as they usually dismiss connecting to their inner being and they keep themselves busy. Women can usually and easily sit still, focus and connect with their intuition more than men.

All successful business decisions men make come straight from their gut feeling and intuition. They knowingly and unknowingly activate it when it comes to business but don't use it for personal matters most of the time.

Intuition is a gift from the Creator. We all have it and can use and benefit from it. As I mentioned, every decision I took in my life, based on my intuition, I was right every time… and the times I did not believe it or ignored it, I was wrong.

TESTIMONIALS

"A year after my kidney transplant, there was a risk of my body rejecting the new organ. That's when I turned to Jocelyne for help, as a friend highly recommended her. Over months, she focused on aligning my body and mind to accept the new foreign kidney. Her efforts not only helped me avoid rejection but also pulled me out of a deep depression. I am now healthy, happy, and grateful to her for her support through one of the most challenging times of my life."

LESSON 5

Intuition is like a trusted friend and mentor who quietly guides us through many twists and turns. It acts as an inner compass, helping us with various situations by offering subtle nudges, warnings, or a reassuring sense of peace and comfort.

Consider a time when you felt an unshakable confidence about the safety of your spouse, children or siblings, even before you had any deep understanding of intuition. This intense feeling wasn't just a random coincidence—it was your intuition working behind the scenes, providing you with a deep sense of assurance and clarity.

Our intuitive abilities are not reserved for a select few; they are innate to all of us. This inner guide is always present but requires activation and nurturing to become a powerful tool.

Trusting our intuition means allowing ourselves to be guided by this inner intelligence and wisdom. It can help us make choices that align with our true selves, adjust our paths when necessary, and find solace amid uncertainty.

So, take the time to activate your intuition, and you'll discover a powerful ally within you. Trust in your intuitive sense, and let it lead you through life's complications, guiding you to a more fulfilling and happy existence.

CHAPTER 6

Happenstance

It started with an unintended meeting, ignited by a companionship that would forever alter my life.

A close friend of mine fell in love with a young man. While she was dating him, I met his friend, the man who would later become my husband.

Initially, it appeared to be a regular introduction. However, as we conversed and shared moments, I sensed a bond forming. My friend's love story united us, and we had been writing our own narrative for a long time.

Reflecting on the past, I now understand how a single moment, one simple introduction, can result in a lifetime of joy or sorrow.

This occurred in the spring of 1985 when our bustling city streets and charming cafes buzzed with energy. Uncomplicated pleasures were the highlight of those golden days. We would go on strolls, talking endlessly and laughing our hearts out.

We had a clear spark of interest from the moment we made eye contact. We were attracted to each other's presence and enthusiastically participated in conversations covering various subjects, from philosophy to contemporary music trends.

It was a new journey. We navigated through our town's narrow lanes and twisting roads and experienced a feeling of connection. It felt like I had discovered a part of myself that had been inactive for a long time.

Despite the gaping difference in our upbringing—he a city child and I a suburb child—as well as in our academic trajectories—he a seasoned university student and I still a fledgling in high school corridors—there was a magnetic pull between us. It was as though an invisible cord between our respective stages of life tied our minds.

I felt like a sponge in his presence, eagerly soaking up the reservoir of knowledge and worldly experiences he possessed. His intellect illuminated the vast expanse of possibility beyond my youthful confines. Each day, every exchange with him in solitude or company was a revelation, an outing into an unfamiliar land where ideas flowed freely, exceeding the limits of age and the academic world.

Despite the difference in our scholarly hobbies, our interactions had an undeniable synergy. On and off, he challenged me to think beyond my comfort zone to explore thoughts I had never dared to venture into before.

Physically, he was far from being my type. Moreover, my dreams of marriage and my own family were beyond my years and his capabilities, be it financial, social or anything in between. But still, as our friendship blossomed into a connection and we enjoyed each other's presence, we began to carve out moments of drives and talks amidst our little social circles.

These city car rides allowed us to go deeper into each other's thoughts and spaces. We even had adventures exploring the nearby mountains and enjoyed the summer breeze during the drives in his Volkswagen GTI sports car.

In those tender moments, I discovered a sense of belonging. It was a feeling I had never known before, and it became increasingly clear that our fateful encounter had set a love story that would survive the test of time.

The seasons shifted, and our love multiplied with an intensity that defied the bounds of reason. In one year, we found ourselves immersed in passion and devotion for each other that hid any reservations or doubts that may have stayed in our hearts.

On the other hand, as a naive and idealistic 19-year-old, I harbored the misguided notion that I could mold the man to fit my desires, disregarding the wisdom that naturally comes with experience and maturity, which I obviously lacked at that age.

In the meantime, my father remained steadfast in his long-held wish to witness my wedding. Potential suitors came, looking for my hand in marriage. Still, despite the marriage proposals from neighbors and well-meaning connections, my mother remained unimpressed due to her high standards and discerning eye.

My mother's decision not to consider suitors who didn't meet her criteria showed her dedication to my happiness and future welfare. However, as naive as a 19-year-old could be, I saw that as controlling and dictatorial behavior.

Surrounded by suitors from good families and financial backgrounds, my heart stayed loyal to the one who had enchanted my spirit. His thoughts and dreams captured me.

I remained unresponsive to the allure of proposals, as my heart was already committed to someone else. The idea of marriage had only entered my mind briefly, feeling more like a distant suggestion.

Our love was a relentless power. I found solace from the outside world in his embrace.

Nevertheless, our journey towards coming together faced obstacles, with the primary issue being the traditional beliefs of my parents. Their conventional beliefs and predictions raised uncertainty about the possibility of our relationship, and it was clear that they did not want us to get married.

Bound by the constraints of tradition and familial expectations, I was prohibited from entertaining his presence in our home or elsewhere.

Then came the secret meetings, with the help of my sister and best friend. They became allies in our budding romance as we were often sneaking away from the watchful eyes of my family. There was no other choice. They were all against our marriage and even our meeting.

Yet, fate intruded unexpectedly, and one day, a phone call, innocently answered by my father, shattered the secrecy of our meetings.

With my heart in my throat, I waited anxiously as the love of my life asked to speak with my father. He confidently expressed his desire to marry me. His words echoed through our home, challenging the conventions that bound us all.

My father firmly objected. "She's too young," he insisted with as many excuses as he could. "She needs to focus on her education and complete her studies."

I felt a mix of fear and determination. I knew this was the moment that tested our love and courage, and I knew we had a long road ahead.

That day, my father summoned me and outlined his reasons and concerns. My father took me aside for a serious talk. He questioned my intentions and asked why I would consider a future with someone still on his educational path, whose future was undeveloped.

"You deserve someone more established," he advised. "You should aspire for more." He also shared his aspirations for me to join him in the US soon, revealing that someone had already sought my hand in marriage for their son.

He argued that I would be better without a partner who was still occupied with his studies.

Little did we know how our parents could foresee what was good for us and what was not, thanks to their lifelong experiences and intuition.

Nonetheless, I sought out my ex-husband that very afternoon to discuss things. One conversation led to another, and we decided to stay back before we knew it. We didn't return home and instead remained at his cousin's place.

Before anything else could happen, in a flurry of decision-making, we decided to get married straight away.

When the news reached home, it was not taken lightly or welcomingly. This decision greatly distressed my father, who refused to speak to me for an entire month.

Yet, we had already decided to get married as soon as possible.

I left home a week before the wedding. I remember that the wedding was on a Monday, which we were not accustomed to. My wedding day was not what I had dreamt of for myself.

My father remained adamant about not attending. Despite his wishes, someone persuaded him to at least allow my sister to attend as my bridesmaid. A few of my cousins witnessed our modest ceremony alongside her. It was a small, intimate gathering, defined more by the people missing than those present.

After our wedding, we remained in Lebanon for approximately two and a half years. At the time, I was concluding my final year of school while he was attending university. Our marriage took place in July, aligning with the summer break.

By September, I was back in school to complete my last year of baccalaureate, and he was finishing his last few semesters of university studies. Once I finished school, I pursued law at the university, while he had about a year remaining to complete his degree.

We often discussed the charm of exploring new lands even before tying the knot, and the reality of living in Lebanon, with its relentless cycles of conflict and instability, only fueled our desire to relocate.

At the same time, my sister-in-law and her husband, who were settled in Dubai, proposed that we join them there. I considered this idea as a primary step towards my ultimate ambition of moving to the United States, a dream I held dear for many years. I was determined to forge my own path, avoiding the traditional route of an arranged marriage in the US that my parents might have favored.

A quiet rebellion simmered beneath the surface in the complex decision-making. It was a rebellion born not of disobedience but of a determination to forge my destiny.

Moreover, the catalyst for this rebellion was an encounter with my neighbor, 4 to 5 years older than me—a chance comment that burned a spark within me.

My neighbor, wise beyond her years, teased me about my future, saying that I should obediently submit to my parent's wishes and accept whatever match they deemed suitable. Her words, though light-hearted, struck a chord deep within me, awakening a sense of rebelliousness I had never known.

At that moment, I realized that the constraints of tradition did not bind me and that I was not obliged to follow a path laid out for me by others. I yearned for autonomy, the freedom to chart my course and determine my destiny. And so, I set out on a journey marked by boldness, courage, and the firm belief that my fate was in my own hands.

I refused to be pigeonholed into the confines of tradition, to follow a pre-determined track simply because it was expected of me.

It was a parting from my previous attitude, where I had declared a willingness to prioritize practical considerations over hearty matters. However, in a twist of fate, I swung in the opposite direction.

In retrospect, it was a lesson in self-discovery—a realization that sometimes the heart leads where the mind does not venture.

Now, after all these years, I teach people to follow the heart and the mind together with a careful blend of intuition and rationality because choosing one over the other might lead to a disaster. When the decision is in coherence with the mind and heart, it is eternal.

Despite my initial intentions to approach marriage with a practical lens, I recognized its transformative power and the control it can have on one's life.

During this time, my husband's sister, living in Dubai, helped me obtain a visa. Interestingly, during this period, her first baby, a daughter, spent more time with us in Lebanon than with her in Dubai.

Caring for my husband's niece in Lebanon became a significant part of my life. She was like my own child, especially since I didn't yet have children. I devoted myself to looking after her with the help of her grandparents - my mother-in-law and father-in-law - who were a tight-knit family unit.

Years later, even after living with her parents in Abu Dhabi, my husband's niece remained close to my heart, and our bond grew stronger over the years.

Despite the distance, we maintained a deep connection, and she became an integral part of my life until she was twelve when they moved from Abu Dhabi to Canada. To this day, my children still tease me that their cousin 'Gissa' is my first child.

More than that, my sister-in-law asked me to be the Godmother of her second daughter. I was so happy to hear that. I felt overjoyed about being the godmother of 'Rhea,' with whom I still have a close connection. I have a deep connection with her now as an adult, and we share similar philosophies on life.

This year, before handing in this manuscript for printing, I was asked by Gissa to be the Godmother of her second child, Sophia, who is now 17 months old.

Again, I was over the moon, proud and grateful to be asked to be the God-Mother in christening little Sophia, who is an adorable, smart and beautiful baby.

This role of God-Mother, which was also granted to me by my sister for both her children Judy and Ghassan, is a crown I wear with humility, care, and pride.

EXERCISE

Whether you are in a relationship currently or single, list all the relationships you had in the past, including the ones you have currently (if you do).

Next, write next to the name of each partner you were in a relationship with, all the negative experiences you had while in a relationship with them and what lessons you learned from the relationship.

Next, identify the common denominator in all the previous relationships—specifically, what patterns are repeated in two or more of them.

After discovering your repeated patterns, write what you would never do or allow in future or current relationships.

This exercise will help you define what is acceptable to you in a relationship and what is not. Make a list of those and keep it in your purse, wallet, or phone to always remind yourself about them.

TESTIMONIALS

"When I first visited Jocelyne, I was in unbearable pain in my arm and hand, to the point where I couldn't even hold my mobile phone. After just the first day of treatment, I felt an improvement, and by the third day, the pain had completely vanished. We continued with a couple more sessions to ensure the pain did not return, and I'm thrilled to say it never did. Thanks to Jocelyne, I am pain-free and have returned to my daily activities without any restrictions."

LESSON 6

We talk here about self-love and how it helps you to not self-sabotage yourself, neither in relationships nor in business or family matters.

You see, self-love is the guide to attracting what is good for you and saving yourself from the hurt and pain in all aspects of life. It begins with being self-aware and accepting ourselves.

This means recognizing our worth, appreciating our strengths, and accepting our flaws without judgment. When we treat ourselves with kindness and understanding, we build a solid foundation for healthier interactions and better decisions.

In relationships, it is our best defense against self-sabotage. When we value ourselves, we naturally set healthy boundaries, communicate our needs, and choose partners who respect and appreciate us. This leads to relationships built on mutual respect and genuine connection rather than insecurity or dependency.

Without self-love, we might stay in toxic relationships, tolerating behavior that undermines our worth. By loving ourselves first, we can identify and leave situations that don't serve us, saving us from emotional and even physical pain.

In the business world, it translates to confidence and assertiveness. It helps us recognize our potential, take risks, and pursue opportunities that align with our passions and values. Believing in ourselves allows us to overcome fear and doubt, common barriers to success.

Self-love helps us set boundaries in our professional lives, preventing burnout and maintaining a healthy work-life balance. It encourages us to seek supportive networks and mentors who reinforce our belief in our capabilities and vision.

Besides, you must know that family dynamics can often be complex and emotionally charged. Self-love gives us the clarity and strength to go through these relationships with empathy and respect. It allows us to communicate openly and address conflicts constructively.

By loving ourselves, we can break generational patterns that no longer serve us. We become role models for our family, showing the importance of emotional well-being. This not only enhances our own lives but also nurtures a healthier family environment.

CHAPTER 7
UAE- A New Journey Awaits

On October 2, 1988, I moved to the UAE, leaving behind my studies to build a new life in Dubai. I wanted to get as far away as possible from the war, which had become almost normal in daily life in Beirut. For me, however, it had become unacceptable and unbearable.

I arrived in the UAE before my husband, and he joined me two months later, on 18th December 1988. I arrived with my sister-in-law's husband and their little daughter Gissa whom I was taking care of with my mother-in-law back in Beirut.

During our time apart, my husband was diagnosed with diabetes. I was completely unaware of his condition until he joined me in December.

As I unpacked his suitcase, I stumbled upon his insulin and syringes, which came as a shock to me. It was a challenging revelation, and I felt a mix of emotions, including devastation and a sense of responsibility, as if his diagnosis was something I should have known about or even prevented.

In the wake of that encounter, a storm of emotions raged within me—anger, frustration, and a sense of betrayal. In these dark moments, I even questioned the goodwill of the divine, feeling as though I had been abandoned by the guiding hand of providence. Such was my train of thought. I was truly devastated at finding out about my husband's health.

However, I soon accepted my fate. I had to. I knew I had to have somehow to deal with an unknown situation, making special meals for my husband and being worried all the time about his food intake and emotions etc.

You know, God always gives you strength to handle new things, even when you think you can't. At first, it might seem completely impossible. You feel overwhelmed and unsure of how to move forward. However, as time passes, something amazing happens. You begin to find the strength within yourself that you never knew existed.

Little by little, you start to realize that you are capable of managing the situation. Each small step forward shows you that you can handle more than you initially thought. Eventually, it becomes clear that God has been with you, helping you all along the way. This realization brings peace and confidence, knowing you are never alone in facing life's challenges.

Now, in our new home, UAE, I found a sense of peace—a sense of belonging—a respite from the turmoil that had plagued me for so long. I was inching closer to a brighter tomorrow.

Soon, we settled into our own apartment and began the search for employment. Even while working long hours, we were scraping by, barely covering the rent and our living expenses.

Hence, in addition to my full-time job, I sought out a part-time opportunity teaching Arabic to young students who needed support with their Arabic language. Of course, balancing two jobs became challenging, but I coped with it.

As time passed, my parents began asking when we would start a family like all parents do. In Lebanon, it was common to conceive soon after marriage, but we waited for around 5 years to have kids when we got married.

The reason I hesitated to have children initially was because, financially, we were not stable enough to support a child. Like I said, we were barely making it work. We needed to work more, establish ourselves more and make our ends meet smoothly and without much hassle. How could we have brought new lives into this world without proper planning and resources? That would not have been fair to the kids.

After two and a half years of being in Dubai, I finally decided to visit Lebanon. It was for a vacation, and during that time, my parents, especially my dad, advised me to grow my family.

Now you can see how fate works. A month after I returned to the UAE, I discovered that I was expecting. I had no idea that I was unexpectedly pregnant with my first child despite our financial concerns. What was meant to happen happened, and I was happy. My husband had some concerns, but our families were delighted.

Time flew by, and eventually, my beautiful daughter, Gaelle, came into this world. She was born in May 1991. It was a blessed day for all of us.

You must know that even before our daughter's arrival, I had planned to give birth in the US and had applied for a visa. That was the initial and final plan, but the Creator had his own plans for me. I could not go to the US due to the beginning of the Gulf War.

Obtaining a visa for the US became difficult for everyone, and my application was denied. Consequently, I had to return to Lebanon to give birth to my first child despite my plans to give birth in the US.

Something else was also planned before my daughter's delivery. I had made a pivotal decision to refresh my academic journey and enroll in university once more. Yup—I had decided to continue my studies, learn more, and do so much more academically despite the demands of my coming phase. I knew that with impending motherhood, there was a persistent possibility that I might not be able to do it. However, my dissatisfaction with not having completed my degree earlier was strong.

Initially drawn towards the study of law, I was eager to examine the workings of legal theory and practice. Conversely, as the reality of my circumstances set in, I realized that pursuing a law degree would necessitate an extended stay in Lebanon. This prospect didn't align with my plans. It was a difficult realization, troubled with conflicting emotions, but I knew I had to steer towards a different path.

It was during this period of contemplation that the guidance of one of my former teachers emerged as a guiding light of clarity. Encouraged by their wisdom and insight, I made the bold decision to redirect my academic focus towards the field of banking.

Yup—I completely switched. Of course, this shift was difficult and new. Better yet, it not only offered me better practical opportunities for advancement but also allowed me to remain flexible and adaptable to the evolving demands of my personal and professional life.

I became pregnant around September, and after being denied a visa to the US, I came to Lebanon in February. Choosing not to give birth in Dubai due to concerns about the hospitals at that time, I decided something else.

I enrolled in a prominent French university in Lebanon to pursue banking. I had to do it during the nine months. Despite being pregnant, I began attending all the classes.

By late May, I gave birth to my daughter. With my exams scheduled for July, I juggled caring for my newborn and studying. You can't imagine what that must be like, but I will give you an idea.

Studying, feeding, memorizing content, changing diapers, getting some sleep for exams, and getting my child to sleep. All of it was jumbled up into my routine. But I remained steadfast. I remained strong and active, willing to do it all, even if at the same time every day.

I remember breastfeeding her while studying. I had my textbooks open in front of me, determined to complete my exams. It wasn't easy balancing a baby and my studies, but I wanted to succeed for both of us. I would hold her with one arm and turn the pages with the other, reading and memorizing as much as I could. Sometimes, I'd stay up late into the night after she fell asleep, getting as much work done as possible. Despite the challenges, I kept pushing forward, knowing that finishing my exams would create a better future for us.

In July, I completed my exams, and by early August, my daughter was around two and a half to three months old. I was delighted to have done so much by myself.

Soon, we returned to the UAE in the middle of a scorching summer since I longed for my freedom, my home and the stability I felt in Dubai.

As soon as I was able, I began searching for a job. I needed it, and it required me to get back into the game as quickly as I could. But it was challenging. It is tough to find employment with a young baby in your arms, especially because of the chores it requires, and I was still breastfeeding then.

Due to financial constraints, I needed to find work, so it didn't matter to me what anyone thought or how things would pan out.

Fortunately, I landed part-time jobs. I was supposed to be working at exhibitions, which typically lasted for three to four days.

Balancing breastfeeding with long days at the exhibition was tough. By then, my daughter was around five to six months old, and I would return home exhausted in the evenings while my daughter was with a babysitter.

Every morning, I would prepare myself for the day ahead, knowing it would be a challenge. Each day was a struggle to keep up my energy. However, I would rush home after work, eager to see her and make sure she was okay. Even though I was tired, I would still breastfeed her, knowing she needed me.

As the days passed, it became a routine. Despite the exhaustion, I managed to get through it because I knew I was doing it for her. Ultimately, the thought of providing for my daughter kept me going until it was time for me to go back to Beirut to attend my classes for the second year of university.

I continued this routine for some time, alternating between Dubai and Lebanon. During the winter months, I returned to Lebanon to attend university, carrying my daughter and her stuff with me, and after completing my exams, we came back to Dubai.

By the time my daughter turned two, I enrolled her in a kindergarten and began searching for a job. Fortunately, I secured a position at a bank, where I worked until 2 pm. In spite of having a third year of university left to complete, I managed to talk with the university to allow me to study remotely since I lived in Dubai and worked at the bank. This meant I didn't have to attend classes but had to be present for exams. At that time, online courses weren't available, so I had to rely on books to continue my education. However, I was determined, so I worked hard.

After three long years of hard work and many exams, I finally earned my university degree. It felt like a huge achievement. First, I faced many challenges. Then, I kept pushing through, even when things got tough. Finally, holding that degree in my hands made it all worth it.

I felt a rush of joy and pride. All the late nights and long hours of studying had paid off. This moment marked the end of one journey and the beginning of a new one. The happiness I felt was beyond words.

After I left the job at the bank, I had the choice of working with an oil company or the local Mercedes dealership. I chose the oil company where it served as a broker for crude oil.

After a few months, I found myself unhappy with the environment. The individual I worked with was consistently aggressive and irritable, which made the workplace unpleasant.

I chose the oil company job over the one at the Mercedes dealership in Dubai because it seemed more stable, but it turned out to be a mistake. The Mercedes dealership `job would have been a better fit for me in the first place. I did not listen to my intuition at that time and took the job for the wrong reasons.

In two months, I received the same job offer from the local Mercedes dealership again. The manager who offered me the job at the Mercedes dealership contacted me again. This German gentleman remembered how I had impressed him with my professional work ethic and dedication when I worked at the bank.

Catering him at the bank, I went above and beyond by doing my colleague's job when he wasn't at his desk, even when I didn't know how to use the banking system for foreign currency at that time. Because of this, he was very eager to hire me for his department at the Mercedes dealership.

This time, I listened to my intuition, quit my job and accepted his offer to work at the Mercedes dealership in Dubai.

All these stepping stones and the plans God had for me, guiding me step by step through it all, were lessons, experiences, and preparations for something greater.

I did not know what the universe was planning for me, and I could not have guessed it either because I knew my ambition was far beyond what I could fully grasp, understand, or even comprehend. The universe steered me in the right direction, and I found myself enjoying the work in this new job and slowly started building my career.

However, unlike my previous jobs, where I finished early in the day, this new position required me to work until 5.00 pm. My daughter wasn't happy about this change at all. She had gotten used to me being home when she returned from kindergarten, and our time together was something she cherished.

The adjustment was tough for both of us. She missed our afternoons together, and I felt guilty for not being there for her as I used to be. This change in schedule made our routine feel a lot different, and it was hard to see her so disappointed.

I had to work because the pay was good. It allowed me to enroll my daughter in a good school and provide her with the things she wanted, as well as the things I wanted for her.

At that time, my husband consistently received a low salary despite having a good job title and doing exceptional work.

Unfortunately, my husband didn't have the assertive personality needed to negotiate for better pay or seek out other job opportunities. Other people doing the same job as him were receiving salaries five or even ten times higher.

Even though, at that time, there weren't many people in Dubai who were experienced in his field, he lacked the personality to ask for what he deserved.

As a result, I had to compensate for his work and make up the income shortfall. Even though it was significantly less than what he could have earned, we still had to make ends meet with modest salaries. There was no other choice.

The pressure of long hours at work was suffocating, especially because I had to cook and help my daughter with her schoolwork every day after work. It was taking a toll on me and my mental health.

Also, by then, I had my second child, my beloved son, Shawn, 6 years younger than his sister.

With my newly born son also needing care and attention, my days became even more demanding. Balancing work and family was a constant challenge. I would feel completely exhausted by 9:00 pm, barely able to keep my eyes open. My evenings were a blur of feeding, changing diapers, and trying to spend quality time with both my daughter and my son. By the time I finally got them both to bed, I was ready to collapse myself.

Despite the exhaustion, I knew I had to get enough sleep to start all over again at 5:00 am the next day.

Each morning, I would wake up before the sun, preparing for another long day of work and parenting. It felt like an endless cycle, but I kept pushing through because I wanted to provide the best for my children. Their well-being and happiness were my top priorities, even if it meant sacrificing my rest and personal time.

It was during this period that I realized I couldn't continue working full days. I had to do something as soon as possible. So I made a difficult decision. I approached my boss and requested permission to leave work at 2 p.m. while continue working on important or urgent tasks from home.

Luckily, my boss, recognizing my value to the company, reluctantly agreed to this arrangement. I was beyond pleased and incredibly relieved. It felt like a huge weight had been lifted off my shoulders. Knowing that my boss saw how hard I worked and appreciated my contributions made all the difference.

This new arrangement meant I could manage my work and still be there for my kids when they needed me most. The sense of gratitude and happiness I felt was overwhelming. I felt a renewed sense of balance in my life and a deep obligation for the support I received from my boss. This decision brought a sense of peace and steadiness to our family, allowing me to give my best both at work and at home.

I was chasing happiness, but sadness was chasing me faster.

When everything in life is going right, there is always something that comes and shakes you to the core.

For me, it was the time when things started to look up for me, and everything on the surface appeared idyllic.

For a moment, we were a portrait of a perfect marriage. The life my husband and I had built together felt stable and rooted in love, but beneath this image, cracks began to form.

Before I became pregnant with our second child, a suspicion gnawed at me. There had been a few unsettling encounters that made me question his faithfulness.

I remember confronting him each time with a heavy heart in the hope that my fears were not a reality.

He denied it all, every time, firmly, with a conviction that made me doubt myself. He claimed these accusations were the product of my overactive imagination that was weaving false scenarios in my head.

I wanted to believe in us, in him, so I pushed aside my doubts. I told my heart that my mind had fabricated these suspicions, that the life we shared was still intact. I believed him because believing the alternative would have shattered what I was trying to hold together.

But denial, no matter how deep, has its limits. His lies and his shifting behavior could no longer be camouflaged.

By September 1997, when he joined me in Canada to help with the journey back to Dubai, things started to unravel.

We were going from Canada to Dubai, and we had our two children—our 6-year-old daughter and our newborn son with us. It was supposed to be a time of family, unity, love, and support. Instead, it became a moment of clarity.

In the way he moved through the days with us in Canada and in the way his eyes averted mine, I knew something had changed irrevocably.

The cracks that had once been small and deniable were now wide enough for me to see the truth clearly, and the weight of this truth sat with me, heavier than anything I had carried before. My husband was having an affair.

My world turned upside down. The harsh reality of my husband's affair dawned on me. The revelation hit me like a ton of bricks.

At first, I could not believe it. I was mad, angry, sad, and heartbroken all at once. The news shattered the denial into a million aching pieces until, finally, I let the truth sink in like bitter poison seeping into my bloodstream.

I knew it. There were signs, and looking back now, I see that the pieces of the puzzle seem to have fallen into place, but at that time, I did not want to see the truth.

I got suspicious that my husband was having an affair first when our daughter was just 4 years old—so young, like our marriage in many ways.

I had decided then, in a quiet and determined moment, that nothing could jeopardize what we had. I shut out the rumors, the whispers from friends or colleagues who thought they were doing me a favor by hinting at things they had seen or heard.

I dismissed it all, believing in him and believing in us. I couldn't accept that our relationship, our life together, could be at risk.

It was not until years later, after the dust of denial had settled that I gathered the courage to ask him directly.

"When was the first time? When did you first cheat on me?" I asked, hoping for a different answer. Maybe I already knew what he was going to say, but his response still hit me like a cold slap.

"You like getting hurt," he replied, his words dripping with condescension. "Always digging up the past. Trust me, it's better if you don't push this. You really don't want to know."

That was the moment I realized, with a sickening clarity, that the betrayal did not start when I thought it had started. It had roots much deeper, going back to when we were still so young—back when he was still at university, and I was finishing my last year of school.

It meant the lies and the cheating had begun not long after our wedding, when he'd come home late, offering excuses that, at the time, seemed reasonable enough. But now, the late nights, the distance that had crept between us back then—they all pointed to something I had been unwilling to see.

His refusal to answer outright was confirmation enough. I could feel the weight of those early betrayals, settling over the years we had spent together, and it made me wonder how much of what we had built was based on a lie. The silence between us in that moment spoke louder than anything he could have said.

You see, when you have a limited income to run the house, it can make things tough for any married couple, especially when both of you have big goals.

At first we started experiencing problems at home, and over time, these issues grew more intense. Things panned out, the physical distance grew, financial troubles remained intact and eventually, the impact surfaced—he began having affairs. Yup, not one but a couple of them.

It turned out that during the time I was pregnant with my son in 1996 - 1997, he was already having an affair, but I refused to believe it and went in denial.

Women tend to do that. When the emotional burden becomes clear in front of our eyes, we seal the eyes completely. The truth becomes too heavy to even pick up on our shoulders so we decide to neglect it.

Even deep down, when we know the truth is all there, we are still inclined toward having more time, having more exposure, and maybe giving more chances for the truth to become a blur or somehow even disappear. But it doesn't. In fact, it only gets concentrated in hue. It becomes darker and darker until it's pitch black. That is when it hits us hard.

"It wasn't until I had my second child, my son Shawn, in August 1997—born in Canada—that I discovered my husband had been having an affair while I was there.

I traveled to Canada in June to deliver my son, and at the same time, I took care of my six-year-old daughter. On top of everything, the pregnancy was troubled with some complications.

The doctors told me that I had antibodies in my system due to a mix-up with my blood type during my first pregnancy.

This oversight during my first pregnancy meant that I did not receive the necessary vaccine post-birth, leading to heightened risks in this pregnancy.

I was taken aback. The danger stared at me, and yet, I could do nothing but hope for the best. The final month and a half was consumed by worry and fear, as I grappled with the possibility that my unborn child was at risk.

While these health issues went on and on, I was expecting my husband to join us in Canada for the birth.

He arrived one day before the scheduled instigated birth and stayed with us for two weeks, after which he returned to Dubai.

Before he came back to Canada to help us on the way back, he decided for himself. It was a decision that he knew would forever damage our marriage.

A few days before my ex-husband arrived in Canada, my childhood friend, who had been my neighbor in Achrafieh, took me to visit a sacred place: Oratoire St. Joseph, which was a beautiful cathedral of great reverence. I brought my children and my niece along, hoping for a peaceful visit.

As we wandered through the different chapels, I found myself drawn to one altar, where I stood praying for our growing family, feeling the weight of the recent changes. My son had just been born, and I was in a moment of gratitude, asking for strength and guidance for the new chapter unfolding before us.

In that moment of deep prayer, something unexpected happened. I had a vision—vivid and unsettling—of my husband with another woman in a way that shocked me to my core.

I had seen these kinds of visions before, too, and the image felt so real as if everything was happening at that very moment. I quickly dismissed it, hoping I was mistaken, telling myself it must be a figment of my imagination. Yet, something lingered, urging me to take note. I looked at my watch and recorded the time of the vision as though part of me knew it was not just a fleeting thought. My heart was telling me something, but my analytical mind fought to dismiss it.

That moment left me uneasy, torn between intuition and doubt, foreshadowing the difficult truths that would soon surface.

I later found out that before coming to me, my husband invited another woman into our home in Dubai. They lived there in our apartment while I was struggling in Canada before the birth of my son.

I was unaware of the woman in my apartment. This betrayal was unknown to me even until after I had given birth to our son, who arrived with jaundice, adding to the already overwhelming stress. You can only imagine my mental and physical state during that tough time.

I was left to manage the early days of motherhood with another 6-year-old child to look after without help.

Despite the emotional disturbance, I knew I had to return to Dubai and resume my job at the Mercedes dealership. Financial necessity drove me, and my husband's inability to fully support us financially meant that I could not afford to extend my maternity leave.

The depth of the betrayal became fully obvious upon my return to Dubai. Not only had he brought this woman into our home, but he had also used my debit card—my salary bank account—to fund over-the-top weekends and staycations with her. I had no idea what he would use it for when he had earlier asked me for the money, saying it was for our home rental expenses.

Discovering photos of their adventures, funded by the money I had earned while on maternity leave, was devastating.

It pulled the soul out of my body, leaving me absolutely numb where I stood, holding the photos in my hand.

There felt no ground beneath my trembling legs, and the air around me turned sour. The skin covering my limbs began to prickle, and no matter how much I exhaled, I couldn't get any oxygen into my lungs. Thoughts ambushed me, and I was suffocating all by myself with the added worries of my children and what would now happen to them.

This series of betrayals left a deep scar on my heart that I could never really get over. Even when my husband expressed a desire to reconcile things between us, the hurt and anger from his continued infidelities—including another open relationship with a different woman after he moved out—made forgiveness and acceptance impossible for me.

How could I?

How could I have dusted such agony under the carpet?

How could any woman let so much pain become invisible?

I couldn't.

Upon his arrival, I confronted him, leading to a discussion where he finally admitted everything. That was a significant turning point for me. This part of my life, though filled with emotional pain and betrayal, transformed me. It showed how our marriage fell apart. Trust was broken, and I had to go through a tough journey to become independent.

I had a serious discussion with him and offered him to keep living with us. When we returned to Dubai for the sake of the children, he and I, as a couple, were done. We stayed in the same house for two and a half years after that discussion in Canada, but we lived there not as a couple but only to maintain peace for the kids and the family.

As the year came to an end, my husband decided to move out on December 31, 2000. This was yet another major turning point in my life. It was a bitter pill to swallow because it hurt deeply. However, it also brought a sense of liberation. I felt like I finally had a chance to take back control over my own life. This feeling of freedom was something only I truly understood. It marked the beginning of a new chapter for me, filled with both challenges and opportunities to grow stronger and more independent.

In the months that followed, I dealt with the weight of my secret—the end of my marriage. I felt burdened by the knowledge only my husband and I had and that my parents remained blissfully unaware of. They had no clue about the turmoil brewing beneath the surface of my seemingly perfect life. Despite my husband's desperate attempts to salvage our relationship, enlisting the help of both our families — my brothers and his mother and brother, the rift between us only widened. Eventually, I reached a breaking point. Unable to carry the burden any longer, I made the courageous decision to confide in my parents.

Finally, freeing myself from the secret brought a huge wave of relief. It felt like a heavy weight was lifted off my shoulders. For the first time in a long while, I could breathe freely. The constant stress and worry began to fade away. With the secret out, I could see a glimmer of hope and feel some peace. Letting go of that burden not only eased my mind but also gave me new strength. I felt ready to face the future with courage and determination. This moment of clarity and freedom was something I had longed for. It marked the start of a new interval in my life.

Yet, my father urged me to consider giving my husband another chance. But I couldn't. I knew deep down that my heart had already closed the door on our marriage despite his repeated attempts to reconcile, to return to the familiar comforts of our home. All his efforts were met with a firm refusal on my part.

In 2001, I learned about vision boards and how to manifest my dreams. This was the same period when my husband moved out, and I remained in my home with my two children and our nanny.

Each night, after my children went to bed, I spent hours reading, doing exercises from the books I read, meditating, and visualizing. I found comfort in small things. These included the little victories. I dedicated myself to personal growth. The small moments of progress kept me going, and the practices I adopted brought a sense of purpose to my life.

Despite everything, I managed to work on myself for several months. Every single day, I focused on self-improvement. I started with affirmations, telling myself positive things to boost my confidence. I also began journaling and writing down my thoughts and feelings to understand myself better.

Visualizing was another technique I used. I would picture a better future and imagine myself achieving my goals. Meditation became a big part of my routine, too. I used to meditate three times a day, finding peace and clarity in those quiet moments.

Books also played a crucial role in my journey. Friends started sending me books that they thought might help. I found myself drawn to certain books on bookstore shelves, ones that called out to me and had a significant impact on my life. These books offered new perspectives and advice that guided me through those tough times.

Through all these efforts, I slowly began to feel stronger and more positive. It wasn't easy, but taking these small steps every day helped me move forward.

A few months later, I experienced a fateful encounter with our company's executive director at the office. This meeting opened the door for me to present my idea for a new department. To my delight, I was put in charge of this new department. This opportunity led to a well-deserved, well-paid promotion for me.

This noteworthy change happened at the end of the year after my husband moved out. It felt like a reward for all the hard work and self-improvement I had focused on over the months. This new role not only boosted my confidence but also marked a positive turning point in my career.

After that, I channeled all my focus on my personal growth and my children. I stayed at this job, and I was happily busy with my responsibilities. I thrived in the automotive industry, which men dominated. I was the only female at that time handling such a position in the UAE.

My dedication and hard work paid off as I continued to grow in my role. Balancing my personal life and career, I found joy and contentment in both areas. This new phase of my life was thought-provoking, but I was prepared and eager to succeed. I felt emotionally, mentally, and physically charged to climb the ladder in the corporate world.

EXERCISE

Our exercise here will be goal setting.

Goal Setting is a powerful tool, and I know firsthand how transformative it can be.

The first time I set my goals in writing, it felt like a turning point in my life. It was not just about organizing thoughts or creating a to-do list; it was about committing myself.

That commitment began after reading The Power of Focus by Jack Canfield, a book that became a catalyst for change in both my mindset and my career. It gave me the discipline to focus on what mattered and helped me achieve goals that once seemed distant.

Now, I encourage you to think about what goal setting can do for you. It's not just about building wealth or meeting a need; it's about creating security. Having your own income is about independence, knowing that no matter what life throws your way, you have the means to support yourself.

You'll never be at the mercy of anyone or anything. This sense of control and freedom is invaluable, and it starts with a simple exercise of writing down your goals.

Let's break this down step by step:

On a blank page of your notebook, write 10 to 12 goals you wish to accomplish in the next 12 months.

Then, set these goals by priority, and ask yourself, which of these goals, if I achieve them now, would change my life for the better?

Keep repeating the same question until you have numbered all the goals by priority from 1 to 10 or 12.

Next, write each goal by priority, the first one on the first page, and each goal after that on a new page.

Next, write the action steps for each goal that you need to take, including affirmations and visualization to help you manifest and achieve them.

Next, start writing the action steps of goal number one as the priority and primary goal. Decide that you will only work on your primary goal starting now.

You will notice after a couple of weeks that the other goals are automatically being activated, and some might even start to be achieved effortlessly. This is the power of goal setting by writing, and when your goals are clear in both your mind and heart, magic happens.

Make sure you revisit these goals often. Adjust them as needed, but never lose sight of them. The act of writing them down and checking your progress gives you accountability and motivation.

By practicing this method, you will create a path not only for financial stability but also for self-empowerment.

TESTIMONIALS

For nine months, I was a virgin bride. I was diagnosed with vaginismus, and it felt like a barrier between me and my husband.

Desperate, I reached out to Jocelyne after failing attempts by my gynecologist and sexologist to heal me and solve my problem.

In a couple of weeks, and after a few sessions with Jocelyne, something incredible happened— my husband and I were able to be intimate for the first time. Without Jocelyne's help, I don't know what would have happened to my marriage.

LESSON 7

Let's talk about mind clarity and how clearing our minds and hearts can help us set and achieve our goals effortlessly.

I want to share a personal story. My journey with my former husband was a significant chapter in my life. Although our relationship was complex and challenging, it played a crucial role in my personal growth and taught me invaluable lessons.

Our time together tested my firmness and capacity for love. Through our ups and downs, I discovered strengths I never knew I had and learned more about myself.

Looking back, I see now that my ex-husband's presence in my life was a catalyst for my growth. He pushed me to confront my fears, insecurities, and limitations. I learned to set healthy boundaries and practice acceptance.

Despite our separation, I remain grateful for the experience and the lessons it imparted.

Through our relationship, I learned resilience. There were times when the challenges seemed impossible, but I persevered. This taught me to face my fears, adapt to new situations, and find a way forward, even when the path ahead seemed uncertain.

Another important lesson was self-respect. I realized that I deserved to be treated with kindness, respect, and compassion. I learned to assert my needs, set boundaries, and prioritize my well-being. This understanding changed my approach to all my relationships.

Making tough decisions was another key lesson. It would have been easier to stay in my comfort zone, but I knew that would lead to stagnation and regret. So, I summoned the courage to take risks and trust in my abilities.

This decision brought a sense of enablement and confidence that stays with me to this day. I also gained a deeper understanding of myself and my values.

Our relationship reflected my strengths, weaknesses, and desires back to me. I learned what I was willing to accept and what I valued and discovered a sense of purpose and direction.

Through it all, I developed a greater appreciation for effective communication and emotional intelligence in relationships. I learned that recognizing and managing emotions, both my own and others, is crucial for building strong, healthy connections.

Ultimately, I came to understand that relationships are a journey, not a destination. Each chapter, including the one with my former husband, had a beginning, middle, and end. While it was difficult to let go, I now see that this experience was necessary for my growth.

Clearing my mind and heart allowed me to set and achieve my goals effortlessly. This journey taught me self-respect and the importance of boundaries and making tough decisions. It shaped me into the person I am today—more aware of my needs, more appreciative of my values, and more compassionate towards myself and others.

Our marriage relationship, though it ended, was not a failure. It was a necessary step in my evolution, enabling me to become my true self and live a more authentic, fulfilling life. I am forever grateful for the role he played in my life, challenging as it was, because it was instrumental in shaping who I have become today.

It is crucial to note that for many years, I have had a good relationship with my ex-husband. We have two children together, and it was essential for me to convert the anger and pain into peace and harmony for the sake of my children as well as for my own sake.

So, remember, when we clear our minds and especially our hearts, we can set our goals and targets and achieve them effortlessly. The most important relationship you will ever have is the one with yourself. Everything else will fall into place.

CHAPTER 8

Reflective

My affection for Dubai is deep-seated and obsessive, often noted by friends and acquaintances in my circle.

Once, a friend's husband remarked in jest, "I wish I knew how they make you love Dubai so much. It's like they gave you an injection of blind love that made you adore it," highlighting my constant defense of the city in social gatherings.

Undeniably, while others might dwell on certain aspects they dislike or issues they encounter, I invariably find myself championing Dubai's qualities and defending its protocols and developments—even in the presence of UAE nationals voicing their grievances over certain aspects they disagree about.

This unshakeable loyalty to Dubai didn't develop overnight. It grew from the connection I felt with the city as my adopted country, the place I chose as a home for myself and my children.

People often discuss the safety and security that Dubai offers, which are certainly significant, but my bond with the city rises above these conveniences.

For me, Dubai represents a refuge. It is a place where I can truly be myself, where the potential to realize one's dreams feels intense. The pain or the joy, the heat of the desert during the day or the piercing cold and wind at night, the diversity, the tolerance, the magnet that Dubai has for all walks of life and ages, and will always be, a home for us, where the losses were too weighty. Still, the gains were uncountable and priceless, too.

It is only here that my healing journey, which transformed my life, unfolded. As a young married woman full of hopes and dreams, Dubai provided not just a backdrop but a spur for personal and emotional growth.

The challenges I faced, including the realization that my ex-husband and I were not the right match, became evident as I got on my path toward healing in this city. In spite of the separation from my ex-husband and recommendations from my parents to return to Lebanon, my heart and intuition firmly rooted me in Dubai. Even when my ex-husband suggested relocating to Canada—where my son was born—I felt a compelling draw to stay in Dubai. My instincts told me that this was where I needed to be, where I should raise my children. And I listened.

I can easily say that staying in Dubai has been a decision I've never regretted. It has allowed me to give my children a life rich with opportunities and security in a place that continues to inspire and nurture our dreams. My love for Dubai is not just about the place itself but about the individual progression I have seen in myself and the sense of belonging it has offered me. I am grateful for everything Dubai has provided me and for turning me into a genuine advocate for the city in every possible way. I am proud of it.

Even back during my married life, right after we had moved to Dubai, I had found myself unintentionally displaying the financial patterns I observed in my childhood. You see, when things were calm and war used to be "on pause," we all, as a family, spent generously and enjoyed all kinds of lavish lifestyles. We didn't let anything stop us whenever we needed to buy something. The minute war was at a halt; we poured out our money like anything. And just when war used to resume, suddenly, we stopped doing it all; everything shrunk, and we seemed to have no money at all, and my parents put a break on everything. So, I learned the same from them.

Much later, while living surrounded by the glitz and glamour of a booming metropolis like Dubai, I was still influenced by the behaviors of my parents that I saw during my childhood, particularly in matters of finance. My parents always had money. My mom loved to keep cash in a handbag that she does not use anymore. Every time she wanted to send me or my brother to the grocery shop, she would say, "Take money from the handbag and go get this and that," However, because of this, from an early age, I observed their approach to money management. This pattern of financial behavior, dictated by the presence of war or the absence of it, brought significant stress into our lives and led me to a critical realization: I was unconsciously mimicking the financial habits of my parents. This was a real wake-up call for me. There was no war in Dubai, so I shouldn't be doing that. But, I had habits; there were insecurities too, my patterns rooted in me, and I personified them because that was my subconscious truth. I have no resistance in confessing that I've mimicked some of my parents' behaviors in the past.

Initially, my husband and I faced challenges due to his excessive spending, which exceeded our combined earnings. He had the same pattern. We both spent blindly and didn't hold back on anything during our marriage, both for our kids and for ourselves.

But later, when I grappled with the consequences of my husband's financial habits, I couldn't help but reflect on my own relationship with money and how it mirrored that of my parents. I could see it. The both of us. The realization that I had unintentionally prolonged certain unrequired behavior was a sobering call, warning me to take a hard look at myself and my financial choices.

In confronting these issues, it became clear to me that my childhood experiences tended to leave a lasting imprint on my psyche in so many ways, affecting not only my approaches to life but also my money, relationships, and self-worth.

Through introspection and self-reflection, I soon began to unravel the underlying motivations behind my financial decisions and to confront any unhealthy patterns or beliefs that no longer served me. It was a challenging process, troubled with setbacks and moments of doubt, but it was also incredibly liberating.

As I worked to settle these behaviors, I found myself undergoing a broader transformation, not just financially but in all aspects of my life.

Gradually, the phase came upon me where I became more mindful and intentional in my choices, cultivating a greater sense of self-awareness and liberation. Somehow, I learned to prioritize my values and goals, seeking fulfillment and happiness beyond material wealth.

Confronted with this, I committed myself to change. I began the hard work of addressing and "healing" these deep-seated behaviors.

You see, this wasn't just about improving our financial situation; more importantly, it was about breaking free from a certain cycle of actions that spanned generations. We never stop it. Whatever comes to us through our parents and to them through their parents, we never even begin to think if they need an evaluation. We inherit them. We take them forward subconsciously, and even if they are sometimes taken along intentionally, we fail to suppress them. Why? Well, they are strong. Whatever we have seen in our childhood, the people we have grown up with tend to have a strong grip on our souls and our subconscious, and if not confronted or healed, they can easily influence us for the rest of our lives.

I couldn't do that. I decided I wouldn't let the cycle ride on. Hence, my goal was to go beyond not only the financial carefulness or the total opposite of carelessness I had learned but also to challenge and change other inherited behaviors and attitudes that were not serving me well. I did this not only to heal myself but to stop the cycle for my children. If not changed, they would adopt the same patterns as me. That is how it works. That is how it spreads and is so contagious that it lives on from generation to generation.

But I was adamant about stopping this. I also learned that all the patterns and inheritance of behaviors, attitudes, and lifestyles can be broken. They all can be halted. It is not impossible despite many people claiming so.

The simplest way to change them is to not entertain them. When I don't entertain them or surrender to these unhealthy habits, and when I ask for forgiveness from people I might have hurt and forgive all those who preceded me, with this action, I don't pass on these habits to my children. One more important action to heal and break those cycles is to serve humanity and help in any way possible, whether big or small, and a deed is worth a legacy. This is how to break the cycle.

Of course, it is not easy. And it wasn't effortless for me either. This process of self-healing and immense transformation involved a lot of self-reflection, contemplation, unlearning, and, every so often, making hard decisions. For example, it was more than just budgeting and financial planning—it was about fundamentally transforming how I approached money. I learned not to chase projects or money anymore; I allow that to show up in my life.

So, eventually, by addressing these issues head-on, I began to slowly bring a change. I began to cultivate a healthy life—not only financially stable but also richer in attaining self-sufficiency and personal satisfaction.

It is basically how I think and feel and how ensuring that the choices I make are consciously aligned with my values and the future I envision for myself and not merely a repetition of the past. Yes, the various events and experiences in my life necessitated a deep and often challenging introspection to address and heal the underlying issues, crucial for me to bring positive changes in my life.

Then, even though I made much money from my job and side hustle, I did not let my children know that we had a lot of money. I didn't reveal this to them directly. And I did the right thing. Though I always took them to luxury hotels on weekends in Dubai and sent my son on school trips locally and abroad and summer football camp to Manchester, I did not let them find out we had much money.

However, after I noticed this scarce mentality and allowed myself to heal, they were already grown up. Their childhood had been spent already. The damage I did to their psyche on this front was already done. However, I also knew that it was now my responsibility to help them come out of it. To help them heal from it.

So, I taught them different lessons about money and abundance. I did this "silently," "directly," and "indirectly" by working on myself first; then I gave them workshops tailored for them. I teach this course to my clients, so why not my children? They had to sit at my studio every day for a couple of hours for a couple of months. I gave them the lecture, course and exercises to follow. It was also a bonding time for us. In turn, it worked out. They changed their perception about making money and attracting money into their lives.

By setting an example and focusing on my own growth and theirs, I influenced their mindset.

Fortunately, my children began to understand the importance of money and how to attract it positively. This shift in perception was a momentous step for all of us, leading to better financial habits and saying goodbye to the unhealthy cycle.

In many ways, I see myself as an unsung hero who has contributed to the well-being of this city, both directly and indirectly, through my extensive network and personal contacts. My involvement has always stemmed from a genuine love and commitment to the city's prosperity. It's a commitment that continues to resonate deeply within my heart. When the government announces an achievement or a new project, my heart is filled with pride and joy that my adopted country, my Home, is successful, the same way I am proud and joyful when my children achieve their goals.

Everyone plays a role, in one way or another, in enhancing or detracting from the well-being of a place. For me, working alongside UAE nationals and consistently defending their perspectives and culture against misconceptions among my expatriate friends and acquaintances has been crucial. Often, these misunderstandings stem from a lack of familiarity with the local customs and the underlying reasons behind certain practices. My role has often been to bridge this gap, educating and enlightening others, which I undertake with a sense of duty and care, believing deeply in the importance of fostering mutual respect and understanding within this diverse community.

Working with UAE nationals on their healing and traumas has been a deeply fulfilling part of my work, contributing not only to the well-being of the individuals but also to their families and the wider community. Often, a consultation that begins with addressing a physical ailment opens the door to emotional and mental healing. This process can have a ripple effect, as one healed individual leads to another; mothers send their children, women bring their husbands, and husbands bring their wives, creating a chain reaction of wellness and understanding that extends beyond the immediate family.

I am privileged to play a role in this transformative process. In my practice, I've extended my healing to include not just individuals but also their living spaces through home alignment—addressing the energy of their houses, gardens, and villas. This holistic approach ensures that healing encompasses all aspects of their environment, further enhancing the therapeutic impact.

My lifelong learning and the techniques I've mastered over the years are applied uniformly to everyone I help, treating each person with the same care and dedication. It's particularly touching to work with the younger generation, many of whom are around my children's ages. They often see me as a maternal figure, trusting me with their most private concerns and maintaining our connection long after our formal sessions have concluded.

Reflecting on the incredible development I've witnessed in Dubai, I'm reminded of His Highness Sheikh Mohammed Bin Rashid's reflections in his book, "My Story." He spoke of his admiration for Lebanon and the UK during his first travels as a child and his hope that Dubai could emulate their best qualities. Now, having seen Dubai's meteoric rise from a desert to a dynamic metropolis, I share a similar hope for Lebanon. I dream of a Lebanon that, like Dubai, respects and supports its citizens with a government that offers unparalleled support and advantages.

Here in Dubai, the respect and support extended to nationals create a society where people feel valued and empowered. My wish is for Lebanon to experience this same level of respect and support, where human lives are cherished, and the government actively works to uplift its people. After all, the suffering and pain caused by the several wars had diminished the hope and energy of people in Lebanon. Most Lebanese who live in Lebanon are depressed, hopeless and helpless. The new generations symbolize all that, and the future for them would be either to stay in their misery or to leave.

This is why I love Dubai. I am grateful for the learning and the opportunities I've had here. While not every moment has been filled with joy, my achievements and personal progress wouldn't have been possible elsewhere. This city has shaped me into the person I am today, and for that, I am immensely thankful. My children have thrived here, and I am filled with hope that their futures, as well as my own, will continue to flourish.

EXERCISE

Practice giving back to society in whatever form you can. It could be money, service, help, guidance, mentorship, or support.

The ultimate pleasure comes from giving, not receiving. While you may enjoy receiving, the real, deep joy is felt when you give.

Offer to mentor people in your circle or even random people for some time. Help someone find a job or support someone in need. There are many ways to give to others.

These deeds will be your salvation. As above, so below; as below, so above; as within, so without. These deeds are recorded, and you will benefit not only from them in the long run, but also your children will benefit as well as their children, and the generations after will reap the rewards too.

TESTIMONIALS

"When I first sought help, I was in a very dark place. I was three months pregnant with my first baby boy and feeling deeply suicidal. I felt utterly disconnected from my baby. I reached out to Jocelyne. From our very first session, I felt a glimmer of hope. I remember being encouraged to place my hands on my tummy, something I hadn't done before. It started to create a connection between me and my unborn child.

Over the next two weeks, everything changed. I began to manage my feelings.

Eventually, I gave birth to my beautiful baby boy. I felt immense gratitude for the help I received. Jocelyne's work is life-changing."

LESSON 8

Let's talk about the positive impact of giving back and how it can benefit your whole family, now and for generations to come.

When we give back to our communities, we create an effect that can influence our family's present and future. Just like the continuous renewal of life, giving back rejuvenates our spirit and strengthens our family's bond.

In my own experience, the journey with my former husband was challenging, yet it pushed me to grow in ways I never expected. It was a catalyst for personal growth, just as giving back can be for a family.

When a family engages in acts of kindness and service, it nurtures a sense of purpose and connection. These shared experiences bring family members closer, fostering deeper communication and understanding. The lessons learned through giving back—compassion, empathy, and selflessness—become integral to the family's values.

By involving your family in community service, you teach your children the importance of helping others. This instills a sense of responsibility and empathy that they carry into adulthood, passing these values on to their children. It's like a cycle of renewal, where each generation builds on the foundations laid by the previous one.

Moreover, giving back helps clear our minds and hearts. When we focus on the needs of others, we let go of our worries and stresses. This mental clarity allows us to set and achieve our goals effortlessly. By prioritizing acts of kindness, we create a positive environment that promotes personal growth and collective well-being.

Consider how everyday acts of renewal, like eating, drinking, and cleansing, sustain us physically. Similarly, acts of giving sustain us emotionally and spiritually. When we make giving a regular part of our lives, we nourish our family's spirit, ensuring everyone thrives.

Involving your family in giving back can also provide valuable life lessons. Just as I learned self-respect through my relationship, your family can learn important skills through service. These experiences teach perseverance, adaptability, and the importance of setting healthy boundaries.

We also gain a deeper understanding of our values and priorities. We see the impact of our actions, which reinforces our commitment to making a difference. This shared sense of purpose strengthens the family's unity and direction.

Ultimately, giving is not just about helping others; it's about enriching your family's life. It creates a legacy of service through generations. By making giving a family tradition, you ensure that your values are passed down, shaping the character and actions of future generations.

Giving back positively affects the whole family, creating a cycle of renewal and growth. It brings clarity, strengthens bonds, and instills lifelong values. When we clear our minds and hearts through acts of kindness, we effortlessly set and achieve our goals, creating a legacy of love and service that benefits everyone. So, let's make giving back a priority and watch as it transforms our families and communities for the better.

CHAPTER 9

Entrepreneurship

You must know that I had already faced numerous challenges way before taking up entrepreneurship fully. This was not my first rodeo, and I was ready with a resolve that was both my armor and my Achilles' heel.

I was a single mother, fiercely independent. My career was a mosaic of roles and responsibilities, each piece a stepping stone toward something greater, though what that 'greater' was remained hidden in the mists of the future.

I remember the days spent working full-time at the Mercedes dealer in Dubai and the nights moonlighting in various part-time roles, each job a piece of the mosaic contributing to my progress and survival. The work was demanding, the hours long and often unforgiving, yet I persisted, driven by the rigid desire to provide a better life for my children.

My decision to go into the restaurant business was born from this relentless pursuit of growth. Of course, it was a leap of faith, stepping into the unknown domain of hospitality and fine dining. Still, with the hope of making a future where time with my children was not an article of trade but a given in our lives, I took this role of entrepreneurship head-on.

However, the reality of being an entrepreneur differed from the dreams. The restaurant demanded everything of me and more, with countless experiments along the way. The hours were longer, the stakes higher, and the balance I sought between work and family life seemed elusive.

Amid the fast pace of managing my restaurant, which often felt like both a main job and a side hustle simultaneously, I found my days overwhelmingly filled with responsibilities. The demands of the business consumed a big chunk of my time and energy, which left me drained and burned by the end of the day.

To counteract this, I established a ritual that became the cornerstone of my week—a dedicated half or full day spent exclusively with my children.

During this time, we would disconnect from all distractions, particularly our phones, and focus only on each other. Whether at home or out for a meal, these moments were precious.

Our gatherings often extended around the dining table, where meal-sharing facilitated conversations. My children and I exchanged stories and insights, probing into both current events in their lives and tales from the past, including my memories from the war and their childhood. This dedicated time strengthened our bond immensely, securing our relationship in understanding and mutual respect.

It was during one of these precious gatherings that both of my children proposed the idea of turning these rich experiences into a book. Yup—that is where this book's idea came from.

My children believed that the stories I recounted—not just of personal struggle and family life but also of broader historical events—deserved a wider audience. Their encouragement was the spark that led to the creation of this book—a project that, after years of reflection and hard work, has finally come to fruition.

As I witness this book being brought into the world, my heart swells with gratitude. I feel so happy to have documented everything I have seen and faced. I am thankful that I listened to my children. It is the power of these enduring bonds of family with them that I am able to do this. I am overjoyed to have taken this step forward, preserving and sharing our legacy with others.

Now, back to the challenges I faced, they were constant, not just external but internal, too. My days were a cycle of chaos, of stress, of exhaustion, and the lingering question of whether there was more to life than this unending struggle.

I was already juggling multiple jobs to support my family as a single mother. My career journey took me from a full-time position at Mercedes to venturing into the restaurant business, seeking greater control over my time and finances.

I was committed to the mission, so I stuck with the tough daily routine, even when it made me miserable.

Managing the daily hassles of my restaurant and cafe was draining and taking me off my path. I felt as though I was merely going through life, disconnected from my true purpose and passion.

The relentless demands of running a business left me feeling down and disheartened, pulling me further away from the path I knew I was meant to follow.

It took me a while, but I got around just like I always do. I realigned myself with my mission—to help others.

It was only by focusing on helping others that I turned my thoughts around. I want to help others in their respective lives by raising awareness about healing.

Yes—I want to put in the effort to promote healing for the people around me. This effort not only supports individuals in their personal growth but also allows me to contribute positively to society.

I've had my fair share of friends, foes, and acquaintances, each contributing to my growth. My encounters with these people, who make up the society around me, shaped me into the person I am today. This is my way of giving back.

This mindset of helping people allowed me to find a deeper sense of purpose for my own self.

How?

By watching others grow and heal.

Watching people turn their lives around for good and achieve their dreams became incredibly rewarding for me. When I could see that it was through my experiences that I was supporting others, I felt content and happier. This motive to help others heal not only helps them but also enriches my own life.

I must emphasize how my commitment to encouraging the concept of healing extends beyond individual transformation. It encompasses a broader societal impact. I seek to inspire others to embark on their growth and self-discovery journeys.

I do this through workshops, seminars, one-on-one sessions, online courses, and community outreach programs. In these settings, I provide tools, resources, and support to get individuals to break free from so many limiting patterns they have and start to live more authentically.

Here, I must emphasize its effect. The ripple effect of this work is astonishing. It has so much power that it extends far beyond the affected individuals. When individuals heal and grow, they become catalysts for positive change within their circle, including their families, workplace colleagues, followers and even the larger communities. Their newfound sense of purpose, authenticity, and resilience ultimately radiates outward, sending positive energy and creating a manifold effect of compassion, understanding, and transformation throughout society. Isn't that wonderful? It is all about raising our frequency, which truly uplifts my soul.

You must acknowledge that this transformation journey and breaking patterns often involve practices. It has to include activities such as meditation, therapy, journaling, and even mindfulness, which helps us gain insights into our undetected behaviors and their origins.

This also includes discovering our emotional wounds and where they come from. This is absolutely essential to restore our perspective on life. When our perspective changes, everything changes, but we start to react to life's tests with more adaptability. We become unfazed in the face of adversity.

This transformation is internal, but it can manifest externally in how we engage and behave with others.

By means of concept, healing promotes a feeling of empathy in our hearts, and in time, we begin to recognize pain in others of similar nature.

Ideally, this understanding makes us build long-lasting, happier connections and more reassuring relationships in place of toxic ones. As we change, we begin to set an example for others, too, showing that adjustment and growth are both possible. This, in turn, can inspire friends, families, and even colleagues so that they can also begin on their journeys of self-discovery, setting boundaries —and healing.

Self-healing improves our overall well-being. This is because it reduces our stress, anxiety, and downheartedness, contributing to better physical health. You get rid of depression in your life.

It is true and proven that physical ailments in your life are linked to your emotional and mental distress. Therefore, by addressing our emotional and mental health, we improve our physical health as well.

In essence, self-healing is about reclaiming control over our lives. It allows us to break free from old patterns, make new choices, and create a life that is more aligned with our true values. This complete 360-degree transformation not only enhances our own quality of life but also contributes positively to the people linked to us through any connection. It also assists our communities by fostering a recovering, more conscious society.

Starting your journey of self-healing is a pivotal step towards living a fulfilled and harmonious life. When we heal ourselves, we truly have the power to influence the world around us positively.

That is what I have learned so far.

When I reflect on the time when I was 19, I see both good and bad experiences. Marrying so early, at only 19 years of age, marked a major turning point in my life. This event not only symbolized a premature transition into adulthood but also brought about a crucial change in my living situation as I moved to live with my husband. This is a big change for someone so young.

This period had the excitement of starting a new life while it also carried the weight of my past experiences and the behaviors I had learned from my family. The move to my husband's place was not just a physical shift but also an emotional and psychological journey.

When I grew up, accepting and healing from these early influences became essential as I took my new role as a wife and someone's constant partner.

By recognizing these patterns, I could actively work towards creating a healthier, more sustainable lifestyle for myself and my new family. However hard and uncertain it was, it was a necessary path to ensure I wouldn't repeat cycles that could hinder my personal growth and happiness in this new chapter of my life.

The instability and abrupt transitions I experienced during my youth and wartime have, in many ways, prepared me to handle change.

However, they have also left unresolved issues that occasionally disrupt my stability. This realization highlights the importance of healing my past wounds. If I neglect to process these experiences, fail to forgive where needed, and hold on to the pain, these ghosts will influence my present circumstances.

It is indeed a journey of unraveling the deep-seated patterns established in our earlier years and reconstructing them into a healthier foundation for our future. This process ensures that the remnants of past conflicts do not define your current reality nor dictate your future, allowing you to live a more fulfilled and balanced life.

Thankfully, I'm fortunate to have gained awareness of these recurring arrangements and have committed myself to actively working through them. This ongoing process of clearing has been transformative, allowing me to gradually let go of the burdens that once weighed me down.

Because of this dedication to self-improvement, I have cultivated a rich network of friends and acquaintances. This support system has been invaluable, providing encouragement and understanding. It's this community that reinforces my efforts, reminding me of the progress I've made and the importance of continuing to work on myself.

I often ponder how I managed to maintain my sanity. At the restaurant, conflicts among staff were common, as were the demands from clients and the pressures from the automotive company to elevate their business.

After dealing with all of this, I would come home to my children's questions and issues stemming from their experiences with their father.

They witnessed things that I felt they should not have been exposed to. However, they refrained from discussing these matters with their father because they wanted his love and approval.

Children tend to blame themselves when a parent leaves, thinking they did something wrong. Consequently, my children felt they couldn't confide in their father about their concerns.

They would come to me, expressing everything they didn't like about their time with him. Unfortunately, their father was not receptive to these discussions and would deny their claims, leaving me to manage their insecurities, fears, and tears alone.

Balancing two jobs while attending to my children's needs left me feeling stretched thin. My children now acknowledge the sacrifices I made, but it saddens me that their memories consist mostly of me not being present at home. They recall instances when I wasn't there after school, but they also remember that I often brought them to the restaurant to help them with their homework before sending them home to shower and sleep.

Reflecting on this, I've realized the importance of prioritizing self-care to maintain mental and emotional well-being. Despite my efforts and sacrifices, there will always be a perception that I didn't do enough.

While my children express appreciation for all I've done, their memories of my absence serve as proof of the differing perspectives between parents and children. We adults may perceive our actions differently from how our children interpret them.

One fine Friday morning in February 2011, my son made a joke during breakfast, and I laughed hysterically. My daughter then asked her brother to tell another joke so that I could laugh again. She said, "Mom, it's nice to hear you laugh. We forgot how you laugh; it's been a long time since you did."

Feeling defensive, I replied, "Don't be silly; I always laugh." But she responded, "You used to, but it's been a very long time since you did." My son agreed with her, adding, "She's right, Mom."

At that moment, the pain in my heart was excruciating. My world collapsed in a split second. All the money I was making, the activities, and the things I was buying for them seemed meaningless. They only noticed that I hadn't laughed in a long time. More heart-wrenching was the fact that I didn't know what 'a long time' meant for them—was it a week, a month, or more? I didn't have the heart to ask them either.

The pain I felt that day still hits me when I remember how much it affected them. It was a wake-up call.

My children are my life, and their well-being and happiness are my priorities. It does not serve me or them if I cannot have enjoyable quality time with them, especially when their father is mainly absent from their daily life.

It was clear to me. I needed to prioritize my kids and my business over the job at the German car company.

That same Friday, at 6:00 pm, I sent my resignation to my boss in Germany. I told him I was giving a one-month notice to hand over my duties to whoever he chose to replace me. He was shocked and couldn't understand my decision. He couldn't grasp it even when I explained over the phone that I wanted to spend more time with my children.

EXERCISE

Dedicate weekly, one day to spend with family, whether married or single. Family ties should be nurtured; they are your support when things go bad.

If you have any issues with any family members, get your notebook and write the forgiveness exercise we did at the end of chapter 3. This will help you heal, set healthy boundaries, and reconnect with your family.

TESTIMONIALS

"I came to Jocelyne with a severe case of hemorrhoids right before I was scheduled for a medical procedure. At her suggestion, I postponed the surgery to give her healing modality a chance. Over 10 days, with sometimes two sessions a day, I experienced a full recovery. It's been a few years since then, and I am still free from any issues. I'm so grateful for her work that I've referred many friends and family to her, all because of the extraordinary results I witnessed. She didn't just address the symptoms; she helped me tackle the causes, a complete healing."

LESSON 9

I want to talk about the transformative power of gratitude. Gratitude isn't just a fleeting feeling of thankfulness; it's a powerful force that can change our lives profoundly. By practicing gratitude, we can boost our overall well-being.

First, let's recognize the abundance that already exists in our lives. It's easy to get caught up in the hustle and bustle and overlook the blessings we often take for granted.

Simple things like having a roof over our heads, access to clean water, and the love of family and friends are gifts. So, taking a moment each day to acknowledge these small yet significant aspects of our lives helps us shift our focus from what we lack to what we have.

Moreover, gratitude goes beyond personal well-being. When we express gratitude, we positively influence those around us. Thanking someone for their kindness and acknowledging their efforts makes them feel appreciated and encourages them to live positively. This creates a more supportive and compassionate community, fostering stronger connections and a greater sense of belonging.

We all face setbacks. It's during these difficult times that gratitude can be most transformative. By focusing on what we still have rather than what we have lost, we find strength. Gratitude helps us to reframe our experiences, seeing them as opportunities for growth rather than as insurmountable obstacles. This shift in perspective leads to greater emotional stability and a more resilient mindset.

Gratitude can also significantly improve our relationships. Regularly expressing appreciation for our loved ones strengthens our emotional bonds. A heartfelt thank you or a simple note of appreciation can go a long way in nurturing our connections. This practice makes others feel valued and deepens our sense of appreciation for the people in our lives.

Remarkably, numerous studies have shown that practicing gratitude can lead to significant physical health benefits. People who regularly practice gratitude report lower levels of stress and depression, better sleep, and improved overall physical health. Gratitude can boost our immune system, lower blood pressure, and reduce symptoms of anxiety and depression. By fostering a habit of gratitude, we can improve our mental and physical health, leading to a longer and happier life.

Writing down a thing we are grateful for each day in our nice notebook for journaling can help us focus on the positive aspects of our lives. On the other hand, mindful meditation on gratitude is a powerful practice that allows us to reflect deeply on our blessings.

We can further integrate it into our lives by regularly expressing thanks to others, either verbally or through small acts of kindness. Do this and watch your relationships improve.

Practicing gratitude is simple and easy, but it is also a powerful practice that can have a deep impact on our lives. By recognizing the abundance in our daily lives, fostering positive relationships, and using gratitude as both a shield and a spear during difficult times, we can create a more fulfilling and joyful existence.

Practice gratitude, and watch as it transforms your life in ways you never imagined.

CHAPTER 10
Jin Shin Jyutsu

My boss could not comprehend that I was resigning because I needed to prioritize my own business and my kids.

He knew that I had already come too far from where my journey started in Beirut, and he was surprised that I was resigning from my post at his company.

The opportunity to work here came as a breath of fresh air in October 2007. I was offered the prestigious position of managing director at one of the supplier companies whose products I had been in charge of while working at the Mercedes dealership. This German automotive company tasked me with starting and building their Middle East branch from the ground up.

Now, this position was an excellent fit for me on all levels. I loved the job; it was prestigious, well-paid, and offered flexible hours, which was beneficial as I was managing my restaurant and cafe simultaneously. In addition, my children were still young at the time, making this job a perfect match for my personal and professional life.

I already had over a decade of experience in the automotive industry working for the Mercedes dealership, and securing this position was a testament to my capabilities.

This position put my life in an even better position, but it came with its own set of hurdles. With time, it presented a unique set of challenges. The automotive industry is dominated by men globally, and being a woman, talking about car mechanics and performance often makes some men feel challenged. While some were impressed by a woman's knowledge in these areas, others were not. Some men resisted my presence and skills, but many supported and recognized my abilities.

Being a woman in the male-dominated automotive industry was an issue for some men. Still, despite the hurdles, I stayed focused and determined to earn respect and prove that women can succeed in any field.

As a matter of fact, during the global financial recession in 2008 and 2009, I generated a profit of 400% for the company, while my target was only 20%.

The Middle East market was thriving with luxury cars, even as the rest of the world faced distress. While our head office in Germany had laid off many employees, I was the only one bringing business to the company.

One day, the vice president of the engineering department called and asked me to repeat an order I had sent earlier by email. The order was worth 1 million Euros and came from one of the dealers from the territory that I managed. He asked me if I was sure that it was a genuine order since he would have to block the workshop to work on such a big order. I confidently affirmed it.

The success I manifested in myself and the company was remarkable, which created some envy for me from colleagues and acquaintances, too. This envy manifested as distractions caused by some colleagues' endless silly behaviors rooted in jealousy and unprofessionalism.

Eventually, the dilemma of whether to keep building an empire for that company while tolerating nonsense or to invest my energy, time, and focus into my own business and my children began to weigh on me. Each time, I had to resolve an issue for a VIP client that consumed my time with discussions and endless calls with my boss, only to reach the solution I had originally suggested—it ate at me more.

When my daughter told me that she and her brother missed my laugh, it was the last straw. I began to envision taking action—to leave behind the income and prestige that came with my job. This decision, made with love and faith, was necessary, as my job had become a heavy weight on my soul, spreading its roots into every aspect of my life. My existence felt frayed by the trials life had thrown my way, leaving me feeling down and devastated, overwhelmed by my struggles.

It was during this time that I felt the need to use my self-healing tool to ease the pain and intense emotions I was experiencing. I had studied this tool for years - My Jin Shin Jyutsu.

I had initially learned about Jin Shin Jyutsu during a sound healing course in 2002, an encounter that marked the beginning of a journey with this ancient art of harmonizing the life energy in the whole system of the human being.

Intrigued by its simplicity and effectiveness, I started applying the basic self-help steps of Jin Shin Jyutsu to myself, my children, my family members, and my friends.

Witnessing its positive effects encouraged me to dig deeper. Slowly, driven by a growing passion, I decided to take the practitioner's course to understand the philosophy and deeper meanings behind the ancient Jin Shin Jyutsu.

At first, I was amazed by the immediate benefits I saw and experienced. This sparked my curiosity, and I wanted to learn more about why and how it worked. The more I practiced, the more intrigued I became. I realized there was so much more to this ancient art than I had initially understood.

The practitioner's course seemed like the perfect next step. It wasn't just about learning new techniques but diving into the rich philosophy behind Jin Shin Jyutsu. I wanted to know the deeper meanings and the principles that made it so effective.

During the course, I was introduced to the history and origins of Jin Shin Jyutsu. I learned about the fundamental principles that guide its practice. Each session brought new insights and an appreciation for this healing art. The instructors shared their wisdom and practical experiences, which further developed my understanding.

During the course, the meaning of self-care and personal growth was revealed to me. It taught me how to apply the principles of Jin Shin Jyutsu to my own life, which was transformative. I found myself becoming more balanced and centered, which heightened my ability to help others.

As I progressed through the course, my passion for Jin Shin Jyutsu grew stronger. I became more confident in my abilities and became more committed to sharing this knowledge with others. The deeper I went, the more I realized the impact it could have on people's lives.

By the end of each course, I felt a deep sense of fulfillment and purpose. I had not only gained a wealth of knowledge but also a new perspective on healing and well-being. I was eager to apply what I had learned and continue exploring Jin Shin Jyutsu's endless possibilities.

This training opened up new perspectives for me and greatly improved my practice. Before, I had a basic understanding, but the training took it to a whole new level. I learned about new techniques and principles that I had never considered before. These new ideas gave me fresh insights into how to approach healing sessions.

With each session of the training, I found myself more and more intrigued. The instructors were knowledgeable and patient, breaking down complex ideas into simple, understandable concepts. They demonstrated how to apply these principles in real-life scenarios, making it easier for me to grasp and use them effectively.

As I practiced what I learned, I noticed a difference in my healing sessions. The new techniques allowed me to connect more deeply with those I was helping. I could see the positive effects on their well-being and the improvements in their energy levels. It was incredibly rewarding to witness these changes.

Incorporating these principles into my practice was not always easy, but the benefits were clear. My confidence grew as I became more comfortable with the practice. I could tailor my approach to each individual's needs, making the healing process more personalized and effective.

The training also taught me the importance of continuous learning and self-improvement since it reminded me that there is always more to learn and new ways to grow. This mindset has helped me stay open to new ideas and keep improving my skills.

Overall, the training was a transformative experience for me. Accidental yet life-changing. It opened my eyes to newer options and gave me the tools to improve my practice. Of course, the knowledge I gained throughout this journey has been invaluable, and I feel grateful for the opportunity to learn and grow. I wish the same opportunity for everyone reading this book.

By 2014, my commitment to and mastery of Jin Shin Jyutsu had evolved to such an extent that it became my profession. Yup— I finally "listened" to the calling. I opted for it as my profession after completely learning the art.

Of course, transitioning into a full-time practitioner allowed me to dedicate myself to helping others find balance and wellness through this powerful modality, turning what began as a personal exploration into a fulfilling career. Now, I feel more equipped than ever to help others on their healing excursions.

Yes—the initial steps were tentative, born out of a mixture of skepticism and hope. I explored the principles of Jin Shin Jyutsu. I was utterly fascinated by its roots in ancient wisdom and its simple yet great approach to wellness. With each touch and each application of this art, I felt as if I were peeling away layers of pain and stress that had accumulated over the years, revealing a core of peace and balance I had thought lost. The transformation was not instant, nor was it always smooth, but with consistent belief and repetition, the changes began to manifest—first subtly, then more noticeably. I was beyond happy.

This art has been my ultimate tool for self-discovery. It has helped me understand the deeper causes of my physical challenges and illuminated the reasons behind many of my actions and reactions. Through it, I began to know myself in ways I never had before. In fact, this modality is aptly nicknamed "Now Know Myself," which captures its essence perfectly.

It's not just about physical healing; it is a pathway to mental and emotional clarity. Every practice, every moment spent with this art, brought me closer to recognizing patterns within myself that I had long ignored or misunderstood. It helped me see the connection between my inner world and my outward experiences, allowing me to heal from the inside out.

This understanding of self has been invaluable. It's as though, for the first time, I truly started to see who I am—not just as a person moving through life but as someone deeply connected to my being, my health, and my purpose.

Seeing the effects on myself, my resolve strengthened, and I extended this practice to my children even more than before. In their young lives, already touched by my struggles, I saw the immediate benefits of Jin Shin Jyutsu.

The nights grew calmer for them, the tantrums became less frequent, and their smiles seemed brighter to me. It was as if the gentle touches and flows I gave them were not only easing their physical tensions but also comforting their little hearts, offering a form of silent reassurance that all was well. It really was.

Soon, encouraged by these personal victories, my journey took on a new direction. The call to share Jin Shin Jyutsu grew louder, compelling me to step beyond the boundaries of my immediate circle.

I began to offer what I had learned to friends, acquaintances, and eventually to anyone drawn to the promise of healing and balance that Jin Shin Jyutsu offered. Eventually, people came to me. And I did what I had to do, what I had learned to do and experienced myself throughout this time.

Then, each session with others turned into a learning experience. For both of us. It became a pooled moment of vulnerability and strength that deepened my understanding and appreciation of this art.

This evolution from seeking healing for myself to becoming a channel for the healing of others marked a pivotal chapter in my life. Jin Shin Jyutsu became more than just a practice; it transformed into a way of living, a guiding philosophy that permeated every aspect of my existence. It taught me about the interconnectedness of our physical, mental, emotional, and spiritual well-being and the incredible power of human touch to comfort, heal, and connect.

As I reflect on this journey, I am filled with gratitude for the serendipitous path that led me to Jin Shin Jyutsu. What began out of necessity has blossomed into a source of joy and purpose, allowing me not only to heal but also to touch the lives of others in meaningful, lasting ways. This initiation into Jin Shin Jyutsu, though born from a place of need, unfolded into a beautiful journey of discovery, connection, and healing that continues to enrich my life and the lives of those around me.

It all started in the heart of Dubai, a city known for its towering skyscrapers and bustling markets, where I boarded a transformative journey that would redefine my understanding of healing.

Under the tutelage of esteemed teachers who journeyed from the verdant landscapes of Europe and the expansive horizons of Brazil to the vast of the US, I was gently ushered into a realm of Jin Shin Jyutsu, where the art of healing transcended conventional boundaries.

These mentors, each carrying a lantern of knowledge lit from the ancient flames of Jin Shin Jyutsu, illuminated a path for me, one that promised not just recovery but a philosophical awakening.

The year 2002 was my introduction to the modality, and 2014 marked the inception of this thoughtful journey. Starting as a quest for personal solace and leading to a fulfilled purpose.

I was torn between work and personal life and the chaotic pattern around me, but as I started integrating the principles of Jin Shin Jyutsu into my daily existence, I felt a seismic shift within. The subtle energies and harmonious balances I learned to evoke and sustain mended the frayed edges of my spirit. Healing, I realized, was an art form of incredible depth and beauty, capable of touching souls and transforming lives.

This personal exploration, rich with revelations and discoveries, soon outgrew the confines of a private journey. The sway of Jin Shin Jyutsu on my life could not be contained or held back; it demanded to be shared, to spread its wings and touch the lives of others. Thus, my role evolved, transitioning from that of a mere practitioner to a herald of this ancient art in the bustling heart of the Middle East. Dubai, with its eclectic mix of cultures and ceaseless quest for innovation, became the cradle for this new chapter of my life.

I took on the mantle of the official organizer for Jin Shin Jyutsu in the region, a role that brought with it both immense responsibility and boundless joy.

Organizing workshops and seminars, I became a bridge between the ancient wisdom of Jin Shin Jyutsu and the modern seekers of healing. Each session was a confluence of energies, a meeting of hearts and minds, where the timeless art of balancing life's energies was shared and celebrated.

This transition was not merely a change in occupation but a calling that resonated with the deepest chords of my soul. Jin Shin Jyutsu, in its elegance and simplicity, had offered me a lifeline.

Now, as its instructor and organizer, I have the privilege of extending this lifeline to others. Dubai, a city that had witnessed my transformation, now observed the blossoming of a community united in its quest for healing.

The journey from 2014 to the present has been nothing short of beyond belief. This role transcended the boundaries of a mere organizer.

I found myself deeply engaged with students, their stories of pain and healing echoing my own. The private session requests that followed clearly indicated that my journey with Jin Shin Jyutsu was evolving into something much greater than I had anticipated. It was becoming a business, but more importantly, it was becoming a mission.

Shortly, over the bustling streets of Dubai, I found myself standing in between the quiet of my studio, preparing for yet another private session. The room was filled with a strange balminess; the air was bathed with a refreshing scent, creating a cocoon of calmness for me in this heart of the city.

It was in this very room that I encountered Mariam, a young woman whose journey of healing would leave an impossible-to-remove mark on me and further solidify my mission with Jin Shin Jyutsu.

Mariam came to me bearing the weight of grief that seemed too heavy for her young shoulders. Having lost her mother to illness, she was wrapped in a shroud of sorrow, her eyes mirroring the penetration of her pain. As she shared her story with me, her voice trembled, but her resolve was clear— she sought help, a possible way out through her sea of grief. It was her story, so similar to my struggles, that reminded me why I had chosen this path.

During our sessions, I witnessed Mariam's transformation as the principles of Jin Shin Jyutsu began magic. With each touch, each flow, I saw a light rckindle in her eyes, a gradual lifting of the sorrow that had clouded her spirit. The art of balancing life's energies, which I had once turned to in my darkest hour, was now a shining example for Mariam, guiding her toward a place of peace and acceptance.

This was not an isolated incident. There was also Khalid, a middle-aged man grappling with the stress of his demanding career and the toll it took on his health. His doubt about alternative healing modalities was real when he first walked into my studio. However, driven by a desperate need for change, he still managed to open himself up to Jin Shin Jyutsu's experience with my help.

Over time, Khalid's skepticism turned into a firm belief—he felt the benefits of the sessions—noticeably reduced stress, improved well-being, and a newfound energy. He was a new man. Witnessing his transformation was moving for me.

Each client who walked through my door, each story of pain and healing, became our collective journey with Jin Shin Jyutsu. The private session requests that followed after the very first clients were the trust placed in me and the art I practiced. I felt so gratified and humbled. It was heart-touching and so satisfying that I could never put my exact feelings into a few words.

As I reflect on these instances in this book, on just a few examples like stories of Mariam, Khalid, and countless others, I am reminded of the power of my work. I am recapped of the miracle I accidentally got to know and then learned. Now, I practice this healing art, and it has become an integral part of who I am.

As we all know, there are no accidents or coincidences in life. Everything happens at the right time and place, guided by a higher force. This journey into healing feels like it was meant to be—a calling that I was led to when the time was right.

One of my clients once told me, "This is life-changing... you changed my life."

Moments like these remind me of the true power behind my healing work. It's not just about alleviating pain or addressing physical issues—it's about making a deep, lasting impact that resonates with people in ways they may have never expected.

These words continue to affirm my purpose, showing me that this path I walk truly matters, not just for me but for those I can help.

My work resonates not just with others but with my soul, confirming that this is where I am supposed to be.

Jin Shin Jyutsu had to become my full-time profession. It was meant to be. It was my calling. It was my miracle. For me, it was never just a job but a natural ability I only had to find out through time and experiences.

Now that teaching and sharing this miraculous practice has taken on a new significance, I aim to spread the healing far and wide, making it accessible to more people who, like me, are in search of support and healing.

At that time, my mission had to develop further. And it did. It grew bigger when I started teaching faculty members at multiple prestigious schools, helping them to work on themselves and helping their students along.

I'm currently working with a community of cancer patients, guiding them on how to care for themselves and encouraging them to find hope and healing. By taking small steps, we focus on what can be done each day to make life a bit easier. It's all about supporting one another and staying positive, even when things get tough. This way, we create a space where everyone feels cared for and understood, assisting each person to find their way.

The influence of Jin Shin Jyutsu extended beyond my professional life. It also reached my home, filling my beloved family's very core. The journey of Jin Shin Jyutsu in my family began as a gentle current, originating from my own experiences and gradually flowing into the lives of my children.

My children, now adults, found strength in the practice from a young age. Ultimately, it became their tool for managing stress and anxiety during their tough times and events. Just a simple act of holding their fingers is a powerful method to help the youth. This practice, deep-seated in ancient knowledge, not only provided them with a coping mechanism but also nurtured a sense of coordination and general well-being that they later carried into their adult lives.

I remember the evening rituals with my daughter, Gaelle, during her exams. The stress of studies and the pressure to perform well would often leave her frazzled, her young mind burdened with anxiety. During these times, we would sit together in the quiet of her room, well-lit by the soft glow of the bedside lamp. I would guide her hand, showing her how to hold her thumb and then each finger, a practice so simple yet so powerful. With each finger held, I watched as the tension slowly melted away from her body, her breathing deepening, her restless mind finding a feeling of peace. This routine, our nightly ritual, became our sacred time, a space where both of our worries were eased and the mother-daughter bond was strengthened.

On the other hand, my son, Shawn, found comfort in Jin Shin Jyutsu in a different way. As a teenager, he struggled with the challenges of belonging. It bothered him so much that the emotional upheaval often manifested as physical discomfort for him. Hence, I instantly introduced him to the practice, somewhat skeptically at first, during a time when words were not enough to channel our understanding. To our mutual surprise, he involved Jin Shin Jyutsu with an openness that opposed his initial hesitation. Holding his fingers, somehow, he found a way to express and lessen the chaos within him and his mind, the battle that words could not capture. In time, this ritual became his silent language of healing, a tool that he would turn to in moments of distress, allowing him to route the complexities of his emotions with self-control.

You see, these practices of Jin Shin Jyutsu are more than just techniques for managing stress and anxiety. As adults, Gaelle and Shawn carry with them the lessons of Jin Shin Jyutsu, not merely as memories of childhood but as integral tools for their respective well-being in life. You can say that it is now a legacy of harmony and happiness that they, in turn, are beginning to share with their own circles.

We still schedule sessions with my son and daughter, and they book a time slot with me to get in the studio and receive a Jin Shin Jyutsu session whenever they feel they need it most.

Reflecting on this journey, I am filled with appreciation and humility. It has been such a great ride. I feel absolutely blessed to have known it. Surely, it has been a bridge connecting me to my children in ways I could never have imagined, acting like a source of strength and liberation for them.

The practice is now intensely built into our family's story. It continues to go on, cultivating a sense of goodwill and safety that can go beyond our generations as a tribute to the long-term power of this ancient art.

In this book, by opening the pages of my life to you, I desire to burn a symbol of hope for those who are wandering in search of light. The ones who are in constant search for healing, to illuminate their pathways that can lead them out of the darkness, and to reveal the relaxing preserve that resides within each of us if only we knew.

My story surpasses being merely my own; it serves as a call for anyone yearning for change and renewal, urging them to take that initial stride into a future brimming with light and inner satisfaction.

Consider this an open invitation, extended with an open heart, to those who stand at the crossroads of their own lives, uncertain of the route ahead. May my book of experiences serve as an escort for you, like a moment of certainty—there exists the potential for remarkable growth and healing. It would help if you believed in it.

Taking on the lessons learned from my journey, I recognized that our struggles are not merely obstacles but opportunities to expand our horizons. This understanding became crucial as I transitioned into a phase where my career demanded more, and my endeavors, like Jin Shin Jyutsu, provided not just relief but the necessary balance that I required in my life.

Growing up in a family where men were considered the primary achievers, I had internalized certain beliefs that a woman needed a man to succeed. These needed to go, too. The cycle had to be stopped.

On the other side, there were instances in managing my restaurant where I felt the need to bring my teenage son to meetings to assert some male presence; it was wrong. It later led me to question why I felt this was necessary.

Realizing this, I focused on healing and forgiving these deep-seated dogmas. I did not need a man to be successful. No woman needs a man to become a successful individual. They can do it on their own, on their terms. I had already proven my ability to succeed self-reliantly in various professional roles, and this only needed to be acknowledged internally.

Besides, I learned my power—the prominence of using my intuition, especially in decision-making. In the past, as mentioned earlier, whenever I ignored my intuition, I regretted the outcomes. Still, each time that I followed it, whether in personal or business contexts, it always led to the right decisions.

The way I achieved all that I have was through a routine or discipline that I established for myself. In the past, I used to meditate several times a day—upon waking, before sleeping, and intermittently throughout the day. However, I no longer follow this routine.

Present day, I engage more in journaling. I set my goals annually and consistently review them, reading and reflecting on them and even visualizing them to some extent.

Moreover, I write down my goals, take my notebook and draft an action plan for each of those goals. I used to set numerous of them, sometimes as many as 101. But now, I've learned to narrow them down. These days, I generally set about 10 goals per year, sometimes up to 12 or 13 if necessary. I focus on one goal per month, dedicating a page to each goal and its action steps.

One of my goals is to publish this book within the year, which will likely happen soon. Fingers Crossed.

This disciplined approach—setting goals, visualizing, journaling, continually clearing, and healing—has been instrumental in my success. The more I work on myself and heal, the more responsibility I take for everything in my life, resulting in lighter energy and a sense of radiance.

This self-improvement has also attracted supportive people into my life and fostered the flow of ideas.

It is a time I find myself drawing people who want to spend time with me, engaging in activities, adventures, and travels. I am happy.

It's also important to define what happiness means personally. For me, happiness is spending quality time with my children—a goal I always prioritized and wrote down. It's about enjoying the company of friends and engaging in activities I love. Happiness will look different for everyone, but these are points worth mentioning in any discussion about personal fulfillment.

The conclusion of this book is not merely an end but a mirror image of a journey marked by adversity and transformation.

From the very beginning, my life was set against the backdrop of war and disorder. Born in Lebanon and raised during a time of war, the early experiences of fleeing from danger, facing near-death situations, and living under constant threat have shaped my worldview, instilling in me a sense of spirit that has become the backbone of my existence.

The journey from Lebanon to Dubai and eventually taking up Jin Shin Jyutsu, a healing art that became not just a profession but a calling, is a witness to the power of healing and transformation. This healing was not confined to myself alone; it extended to my children, influencing their lives and choices and, through my teachings, to the lives of many others seeking solace and healing.

My story is about how adversity can lead to a deeper understanding of oneself and others, fostering an empathetic approach to life's challenges. It is about the importance of forgiveness and gratitude, themes that recur throughout the story and cannot be overstated. These powerful acts of healing have opened new doors and pathways in my life, allowing me to move beyond past hurts and grasp new opportunities, whether dealing with personal betrayals or professional setbacks.

This book is also a celebration of the power of maternal love and the bond between a mother and her children. Despite the hardships and the distances, the connection with my children remained unbreakable, guiding many of the decisions and choices I made. Their independence and successes are a source of immense pride and joy, highlighting the enduring influence of a mother's love and guidance.

As I reflect on my journey from the war-torn streets of Lebanon to finding a new life and purpose in Dubai, I am reminded of the transformative power of forgiveness and love. These experiences have not only shaped me into the person I am today but have also imbued me with a deep sense of purpose and a desire to help others heal and find their path to fulfillment.

So, you can say that my mission is to spread the word of Jin Shin Jyutsu because I believe that when every person works on themselves and rebuilds and improves their lifestyle, everyone around them benefits—it has an effect. So, by improving your lifestyle, behavior, and attitude toward those around you—like your family, friends, and colleagues—each individual's actions can collectively lead to harmony for one and all. I've touched on this previously as well, but I feel that it's a topic that merits either the opening or concluding chapter of my book, as it truly condenses my mission.

Currently, I'm dedicated to expanding the influence of Jin shin Jyutsu even more. I share daily videos on social media to teach people how to manage various physical, mental, and emotional challenges. My objective is to extend this teaching to schools, centers, and government departments. The more people can work on clearing negativity from themselves, the better for everyone. This passion drives my current focus, and I'm actively working on my book, flashcards, and recording online courses while continuing to heal and clear any negativity I encounter. What comes next, I'm not sure, but for now, I'm concentrating on these initiatives.

Even clients who come to me with physical problems often end up addressing emotional issues. Many people are dealing with depression and reliance on antidepressants, which has become another focus for my efforts—to help them overcome these challenges.

The book's purpose is to share my story, not as a biography, but as an example of how I steered out of negative situations, built my career, opened my business, and supported my children and my healing. Through Jin Shin Jyutsu—a Japanese healing modality that has become my profession—I've found a powerful tool for personal and professional growth.

Ultimately, the book aims to show how, from struggle, you can achieve something remarkable. It details the journey I've been through, the pain and negativity I've overcome, and how I used these experiences to better my life and that of my children.

The painful stories of war I shared, the betrayal of a cheating husband, the countless challenges at work and in business—these are not just chapters in my life; they are experiences meant to show you something deeper. No matter how tough, heartbreaking, or overwhelming the situation may seem, you can overcome it. These moments, while painful, are opportunities to rise, to learn, and to transform.

If I could find my way through the darkest times, you can too. I have learned that strength does not come from avoiding difficulty; it comes from facing it head-on.

Every challenge holds the potential for growth. You are not defined by what happens to you but by how you respond to it.

If I could move forward and heal, you absolutely can do the same. Trust that within you lies the power to not only survive but to thrive.

I am a complex personality, just like everyone else. The difference now is that I dare to admit it.

In the past, if someone said, "You're not an easy person," I would take offense. But really, who is?

Yes, I'm complex. But complexity does not mean contradiction—it means depth. I am courageous, yet I move with caution. I am compassionate, yet at times I find myself indifferent. Throughout my childhood, I was obedient, and yet, in later years, rebellion found its way into my spirit.

I am both calm and quiet, yet at the same time, bubbling with ambition and movement. These seemingly opposing qualities coexist within me, and that's okay. They don't cancel each other out—they define who I am.

Is this complexity a result of the wars I have lived through?

Is it my genetics, my upbringing, or the unique blueprint I carry within me?

Perhaps it is a mix of all these things. Every experience, every challenge, every joy and sorrow has woven these threads into the fabric of who I am. But instead of viewing my complexity as something to hide or explain away, I now see it as something to embrace. It is through these layers, these contradictions, that I have found strength, resilience, and a deeper understanding of myself.

Ultimately, this is the journey we are all on to unravel, understand, and accept the complexity within us so we can live authentically, free from the weight we have carried for so long.

I hope you enjoyed the journey and learned something to help you reflect on your own life and get motivated to heal and change your life for the better.

Wherever you are in your life right now… striving always for a better tomorrow is the key to happiness and joy. Always remember that the light within you will always conquer the darkness within.

EXERCISE

Write in your nice notebook your values about money, family, business and anything that defines you as a person, mother, father, colleague, friend, or partner.

Then, start eliminating the most unimportant values for you, those you can live without and let go of.

When you reach the last two values, drop one that is not as important as the one you will keep.

Know that the values you keep are what define you and dictate your decisions in life.

TESTIMONIALS

"I came to Jocelyne with a desperate mind to feel better after being diagnosed with depression and was grieving the loss of my father to cancer.

At the first session, I was planning to leave and never come back to her. But the following day, something brought me back, so I had a second session with Jocelyne. After every session, something was shifting, I felt lighter, and my heart opened. From that moment on, I always say I was born twice in this life: once when my mother gave birth to me, and the second time when Jocelyne healed me and gave me purpose and life again.

LESSON 10

My whole life story was about resilience, self-awareness, compassion and perseverance. These ideas have been constant companions in my life, helping me through tough times and strengthening me.

Think of resilience as a lifelong friend who is always there. Whether it's a physical challenge or a tough situation, we must bounce back, recover, and thrive. Life throws us many illnesses, obstacles, and losses. Each of these experiences tests our mental strength and ability to handle adversity. It is not just about surviving hard times; it's about being mentally and emotionally flexible. It's about having a mindset that is open and willing to learn from failure. It's about determination, perseverance, and hope that helps us overcome even the hardest challenges.

When we face challenges, we confront our limitations, fears, and doubts. We are pushed to the edge of our comfort zones, and it's there that we find our inner wisdom.

Resilience teaches us to let go of the past and live in the present. It helps us with uncertainty and find our way through adversity. We learn to trust, have faith, and hope, which carry us through the toughest times. It is a tool for growth and transformation. It helps us discover our true potential and become the best versions of ourselves. It's a gift that allows us to grow, evolve, and thrive in a constantly changing world.

Self-awareness is another important part of this journey. Every experience offers a chance to learn and grow, whether a success or a setback. Understanding yourself, your strengths, and your weaknesses is crucial for making good decisions and confidently handling life.

It helps you recognize your thoughts, emotions, and actions. By acknowledging your limitations and vulnerabilities, you can improve yourself and make positive changes in your life. With self-awareness, you can identify your passions and values and align them with your goals. This clarity helps you make decisions that reflect your true self, leading to a more fulfilling life.

It also helps you develop emotional intelligence, which is key for building strong relationships and social situations. By understanding your emotions and those of others, you can communicate more effectively and empathetically.

Recognizing your strengths and weaknesses helps you improve your skills, leading to personal and professional success.

Faith and surrender also play a big part in this journey. Trusting a higher power helps us find comfort and perspective, knowing that some things are beyond our control. This understanding lets us let go of the need for control and live in the moment.

Faith gives us hope in darkness and reminds us that we are not alone. It gives us the strength to persevere through difficult times and emerge stronger and wiser.

Spiritual connections bring peace and clarity, helping us see the world in a new light. Life's struggles are not punishments but opportunities for growth and learning.

Trusting in a higher power allows us to go with the flow of life. We learn to trust in the natural flow and surrender to a higher power's will.

In the end, life is full of twists and turns, unexpected challenges, and surprises. But every experience holds the potential for growth, learning, and transformation. Just like the seasons change, we can too. Every ending marks a new beginning full of promise and possibility.

In the darkness, find the light. It's in our struggles that we discover our greatest strengths and wisdom. Life may be unpredictable, but how we respond is what truly matters. Hug the unknown, adapt, and evolve. This way, we discover our capacity for renewal and growth.

Remember, every storm will pass, and the sun will shine again. Hold on to hope and trust that better days are ahead. In the stillness of the night, listen to your heart. There, you will find wisdom, courage, and guidance. You are stronger than you think, braver than you feel, and capable of more than you imagine. Face your fears and chase your dreams. In doing so, you will discover the immense potential within you.

Life is a mix of ups and downs, twists and turns. Every experience is an opportunity to learn, grow, and become the best version of ourselves. In the midst of chaos, find the calm. It's in stillness that we discover our inner strength and deepest wisdom.

Remember, every experience, no matter how difficult, holds the potential for transformation and growth. Clasp the journey, trust the process, and know you can overcome anything.

You are a warrior, a survivor, and a thriver!

ABOUT THE AUTHOR

Jocelyne Chidiac

- Certified Jin Shin Jyutsu Practitioner

- Instructor

- Home Alignment Expert

- Feng Shui Specialist

- Flying Stars Specialist

Jocelyne Chidiac has transformed Jin Shin Jyutsu therapy in the Middle East. Her journey to find balance, fulfillment, and purpose in all areas of her life inspired those around her. As more people sought her guidance, she dedicated herself to spreading joy, healing, and harmony. This became her mission, and she committed to sharing her knowledge and helping others improve their lives, both personally and professionally. Over time, she became a symbol of hope and transformation for many.

Her unique approach earned her recognition, and she became a certified Jin Shin Jyutsu practitioner and instructor.

Today, with more than 24 years of experience in Jin Shin Jyutsu and a decade in personal development, Jocelyne specializes in helping clients work through trauma, depression, and relationship issues. She also supports them in managing their mental and emotional well-being, especially during illness and recovery.

In addition to her healing work, Jocelyne is a dedicated success coach. She helps people set and achieve their career goals, working holistically to unlock their potential and remove any barriers that stand in their way. Her knowledge extends to other areas like Home Alignment, Feng Shui, and Flying Stars. By combining these practices, she ensures her clients achieve the best results, helping them create lives filled with balance and harmony. After helping thousands of clients over the years, Jocelyne has become a trusted guide for those looking to heal and change their lives.

Jocelyne's career began in the automotive industry, where she has over 25 years of experience in management and business development. Her entrepreneurial spirit allowed her to successfully set up and transform businesses, particularly in the automotive and retail sectors.

Her journey in the automotive field took off when she joined Gargash Enterprises in April 1994. There, she started a new department called The Styling and Performance Centre for Mercedes-Benz. She led a team focused on the growing business of customized luxury cars and managed local modifications for existing cars. Under her leadership, the sales of customized cars doubled, benefiting the company's workshops and parts department.

Later, Jocelyne was appointed as the Managing Director for the Middle East by Brabus GmbH, a global leader in high-performance supercars and customized Mercedes-Benz vehicles. She established Brabus Middle East, setting up their branch, including flagship offices, showrooms, and workshops. In just three years, she transformed the business, increasing Brabus sales in the Middle East by 400% compared to the years before her arrival.

Jocelyne has lived in Dubai since October 1988 and she continues to enjoy her life with both her children there.